Pathways to participation

Pathways to participation

JOHN E. HEBDEN
Senior Lecturer, Department of Business and Administration,
University of Salford.

GRAHAM H. SHAW
Senior Consultant, Industrial Training Service

A HALSTED PRESS BOOK

JOHN WILEY & SONS
New York – Toronto

PROPERTY OF
CLACKAMAS COMMUNITY COLLEGE

English language edition, except U.S.A. and Canada published by
Associated Business Programmes Ltd,
17 Buckingham Gate, London, S.W.1

Published in U.S.A. and Canada by
Halsted Press, a Division of
John Wiley & Sons Inc
New York.

First published 1977

Library of Congress Cataloging in Publication Data

Hebden, John, 1939–
Pathways to participation

"A Halsted Press Book."
1. Employees' representation in management —
Great Britain. I. Shaw, Graham, Keith, joint author.
II. Title.
HD5660.G7H4 1977   658.31'52   77-8207

ISBN 0-470-99196-8

© J. Hebden and G. Shaw

Typeset by
Computacomp (UK) Limited, Fort William, Scotland
Printed and bound in Great Britian by
Redwood Burn Limited, Trowbridge & Esher

Contents

43855

Introduction

It has become a commonplace to say that we live in a society dominated by change – but it is nonetheless true.

We see about us the *physical* manifestations of change: in our environment, in our cities, in patterns of housing and in modes of transport. Changes in our work environment affect us crucially: changes in forms of ownership, changes in size, changes in technology and changes in organisational structure.

But perhaps the most important changes have occurred in *attitudes* and *values* throughout the industrial world and among the newly industrialising nations. A basic shift in values has occurred towards authority. We have gradually lost the outward unity that the Church once imposed as the arbiter of moral standards and we have not produced an alternative institution to carry out this function. It is not that we have failed to do this – we have not wanted to try. This is not to suggest a view of pre-industrial times – or even of early industrialism – in which there was no conflict or dispute. But today such actions and sentiments are more likely to be seen as *legitimate*.

Major groups in our contemporary industrial society are characterised by a reluctance to accept authority as divinely given or emanating from birth or the possession of wealth and property. The democratic ideal gives every man an equal say. Even the most recent fascination in our meritocratic society, the respect for the authority of 'the expert', is giving way to scepticism by some and outright rebellion by others. The words of planners and politicians, of accountants and managers, of architects and engineers have been found to be fallible and capable of refutation. The many successes of such experts are lost in the irreverence promoted by well publicised failures. The closure of school buildings while high alumina cement is checked, the costs associated with the computerisation of driving licences and vehicle registration, the social problems following thirty years of urban renewal and the failure of the British economy to keep pace with that of our closest competitors are but examples of the kind of events that are leading to a disenchantment with experts and a demand for the greater involvement of the 'ordinary man' in their decisions.

Such a demand for involvement should not be surprising. The education system, for example, exists not just to produce the workers of the next generation, but to develop and stretch the minds of people. It is successful to the extent that it develops in people a fine critical faculty. We cannot expect to train people in this way and expect them thereafter to accept unquestioningly the dictates of others.

A further commonplace comment on our society is that we are increasingly dominated by the activities of large, complex organisations, and bureaucracies. Such organisations have taken over whole areas of our lives. From hospitals to holiday tour companies, from comprehensive schools to polytechnics and universities we find we must deal with bureaucratic forms of organisation. The provision of local authority services, of public utilities, of banking and insurance are, it seems, inevitably administered through complex organisations on a large scale.

A reaction to the growth of bureaucracies and the apparent power of the expert has been the seizure by 'ordinary people' of forms of involvement. Action groups have protested, sometimes successfully, against airport and motorway proposals, against poor housing and schooling and against the closure of factories, shipyards and newspapers. To some extent 'authority' has recognised the validity of these actions and has established institutions to cater for them. In England some local authorities have established neighbourhood and community councils and in Scotland there is legal provision for them.* The growth of parent-teacher associations, of community health councils and of consumer councils are similar evidence of the beginning of a process of greater involvement on a variety of subjects.

The central concern of this book is with complex organisations, conceived as *work* organisations, i.e. as organisations which, in order to pursue their objectives, employ people. As in other areas, the demand by people for greater levels of involvement in decisions at their place of work is being expressed through direct action. We believe this is a *partial* explanation of strikes, of factory occupation, of labour turnover and low productivity. To some extent such involvement in work-place decisions has been catered for by trade unions and collective bargaining. But how do we ensure involvement in trade union organisation? In any case, the bargaining role places workers in the position of opposing. It provides too easily what Wellens calls 'negative participation'[1] but less easily a positive initiative for the running of the organisation.

We believe that organisations of all kinds – not just industrial or commercial companies – will be obliged, if they are to remain effective˙ and competitive, to provide some means of permitting their members to participate more in the process of decision-making. This should not be a response to legal prescriptions but to the demands of an

---

* Neighbourhood and community councils exist, for example, in Liverpool, Stockport and Lambeth. Legal provision for community councils is made under the Local Government (Scotland) Act, 1973.

educated labour force for greater influence over their work situation.

In the chapters that follow we do not suggest a single prescription that will achieve such participation, but some alternative pathways available. We begin by exploring in more depth what we mean by participation and by establishing a framework within which different participative forms have been accommodated. These different forms are considered in Chapters 2, 3 and 4. In Chapter 5 we examine the constraints that limit and that foster participation. Finally, in Chapters 6, 7 and 8 we discuss the means by which participation may be implemented, the opportunities that some situations offer and the pitfalls that can be encountered. The various themes that are developed are drawn together in conclusion where we consider the prospects for participation.

References

1. J. Wellens, *Worker Participation: A Practical Policy*, Wellens Publishing (Guilsborough 1975), p. 12.

1 Perspectives on participation

Introduction

Participation is an overarching concept which includes a variety of forms and practices. Included among these are practices associated with industrial democracy, with the enlargement and enrichment of operational tasks and with management styles which seek to improve effectiveness through the involvement of workers at all levels in decision-making processes.

As several writers have noted, participation exists as a matter of fact in all organisations. Wellens, for example, says that 'through putting in their skill, time and effort the workers are already participating in a very real sense in the production of those goods and services which their company markets'.[1] We would go further than this and suggest that such participation also requires an element of decision-making by workers. Alan Fox has pointed out the fallacy of seeing decision-making as a solely managerial activity.[2] Decision-making is the process of choosing between alternatives and the extent to which individuals are free to do this, the extent to which they are free to exercise discretion, is the extent to which they participate. Viewed in this way, the critical question is not whether there should be participation, but how far it should be extended; not *if* but *how much*.

Participation in decision-making has been restricted in

several ways up to the present. Decision-making concerned directly with the workers' jobs has been restricted and delineated by engineering design which has aimed to reduce the amount of variability that may be attributed to individual workers. Involvement in broader and more far reaching managerial decisions has been restricted and delineated by organisational design which provides for greater discretion in decision-making at the upper levels of the management hierarchy.

Such formal attempts to restrict the participation of individuals in decision-making, however, have been met by informal measures to circumvent them and by open confrontation between the parties affected. Nowadays, for example, decisions cannot be taken in the work-study office and then imposed. Informal practices may arise to defeat the best thought out plan and increasingly it is the case that work-study schemes are subject to negotiation before they are accepted by the workers involved. Higher levels of decision too, cannot easily be made and implemented unilaterally. Informal attempts will be made to influence such decisions and, where they vitally affect the self-interest of other groups, may ultimately be opposed and rejected or significantly amended.

When we talk of introducing participation, we are in reality talking of the extension, the recognition or the formalisation of participation. The greater involvement of people in decisions at all levels of the organisation should lead, not only to more effective decisions by allowing for the input of further relevant information, but should also avoid the time-consuming and sub-optimising processes involved in negotiations after decision-making in order to get decisions implemented.

The process of participation is a social process ensuring that decisions are taken in a social context. Decision-making involves many forces. The man on the assembly line who participates in the manufacturing process by means of various formally restricted and highly routinised decisions is sharing his decision-making with designers, industrial engineers, production management and quality control. The latter groups contribute to the daily decisions that the worker takes by establishing criteria within which he must operate. The shape, colour and constituency of the product, the means of manufacture, the speed of output and its cost, the acceptable limits of quality may all be decided in advance. Conventional management practice has sought to reduce the span of discretion left to the individual worker as far as possible by the prior decisions of a variety of experts.

In practice, workers may seek to modify these decisions in their own interests. Within the current debate on participation is a recognition that the process of unilateral, specialist decision-making has gone too far. Participation in decision-making, it is suggested, must be restructured to ensure that fewer individuals are left with small, meaningless areas of discretion and the alternatives of docile acquiescence, militant opposition, or uncontrolled adaptation.

The reversal of the trend, however, involves more than the relative amounts of discretion. It involves the social process by which incremental parts of the total decision are contributed. Again, to paraphrase conventional management wisdom, constituent parts of the total decision are made individually by specialists at different places and at different points in time. Increasing participation in decision-making involves not simply the readjustment of different amounts of decision contributed by one individual or another; it involves bringing together different parts of the total and thus reversing the process of fragmentation.

It is the social or inter-personal nature of the participative process that provides the main element of our definition of participation. Participation involves several people who influence decision outcomes. However, not all commentators have been satisfied with the idea of 'influence'. Guest and Fatchett, for example, dismiss 'influence' as lacking precision and being difficult to quantify.[3] They suggest that 'a definition of participation which emphasises *control* is most useful in any attempt to study participation meaningfully'.[4] Tannenbaum similarly places control at the centre of his definition. Participation, he says, 'refers to the formal involvement of members in the exercise of control, usually through decision-making in group meetings'.[5] Tannenbaum, however, sees little distinction between control and influence. The terms, he notes, are 'sometimes used interchangeably' and he subsequently uses the terms in this way himself.[6]

We would suggest that the distinction between these words is more than an exercise in semantics. Our use of the term 'influence' rather than 'control' is connected with more than the methodological problems of quantifying one term as against another. Treating the terms as synonymous can give rise to the kind of ambiguities that arise from Tannenbaum's own definition. Control, he suggests,

> 'refers to any process in which a person or group of persons or organisation of persons *determines, that is intentionally affects*, the behaviour of another person group, or organisation'.[7] (Italics added).

We suggest that the processes of *determining* and *intentionally affecting* contain important differences. If one determines an outcome, then one's control is absolute. It can be conducted without the presence of other parties. If one affects, then one's control is not necessarily absolute. Other parties may also affect and the outcome will then be some middle position. The latter may be called partial control or, more recognisably, influence. The distinction between control and influence is that the former permits unilateral action by one party, the latter occurs in a social setting in which several parties may participate. Poole notes in this regard that

situations where management effectively exerts
control cannot be synonymous with fully-fledged
participation in decision-making and, similarly, that
participation must itself be incompatible with genuine
workers' control.[8]

Although we would not in theory press the argument this
far (it is presumably possible for workers or managers to
participate solely in certain decisions), for the most part, in
the situation as it now exists, participation is likely to be a
process of co-decision by more than one party. It seems
likely in the foreseeable future to be a process of mutual,
though not necessarily equal, influence on a range of
organisational decisions.

Participation therefore, whatever the objectives of its
proponents, must affect the degree of power that can be
exercised by different parties. Our emphasis on influence
rather than control reflects our view of what has been
involved in most schemes of participation to date and what
is likely to be achieved in the near future. For the most part
these schemes concern incremental changes in the
distribution of organisational power rather than radical and
fundamental re-allocations.

This brings us close to the definition provided by French
and his colleagues when they say that

'participation refers to a process in which two or more
parties influence each other in making certain plans,
policies and decisions'.[9]

This definition not only focuses on marginal changes in the
distribution of power, it also concentrates on the *processual*
aspects of participation. In thus concentrating on the
process, however, we would not wish to ignore the
institutional structure within which the process occurs.
Nevertheless the core of the concept of participation lies in

the kind of interpersonal relationships that come to characterise participative organisations. If participation was simply about getting the structure right, it could be established, disestablished and reestablished at will. Because it is about the relationships between people, it cannot be chopped and changed but needs careful forethought, careful planning and, once started, whole-hearted support to make it work. The introduction of participation, because it changes relationships, changes expectations of those relationships. If expectations are raised but not fulfilled, then the organisation may be in a worse position than had it never tried.

This is not to deny the importance of structure. Structure gives form and shape to the changed relationships. But structure should not get ahead of the new expectations, raising them to levels that cannot be fulfilled; nor should it strangulate new relationships. Structures should be flexible enough to permit a steady growth and development of new forms of participative decision-making. The building of the new relationships must take time. The establishment and testing of confidence is hard to build and easy to destroy. A knowledge of and agreement over, the direction that is to be taken will avoid establishing false expectations of what can be achieved and the subsequent disillusionment. In these situations, while 'objective participation' may be considerable, disappointed expectations may result in a low level of 'psychological participation', of perceived participation by the parties involved.

Organisational perspectives

This approach to participation which emphasises the role of influence on organisational decision leads to a discussion of the nature of relationships within complex organisations and in particular to the interrelated concepts of organisational power and conflict.

Power is a feature of all complex organisations and refers to the ability of superiors to influence the actions of subordinates in accordance with their (the superiors') intentions. The power of superiors may be essentially coercive, resting, for example, on physical or economic threats. The basis of such power may be concealed in that the threats are rarely, if ever, carried out because subordinates conceive of the power as being legitimate and do not challenge it. Sociologists describe such legitimate power as 'authority' and it is interesting to note that the legitimation of managerial power lies in large part in the views that workers hold of managerial power. A major preoccupation of management, as of all power elites in a variety of settings, is concerned with persuading workers and other subordinates of the legitimacy of their power. As Richard Hyman puts it, a 'significant form of power is the ability to preclude opposition from even arising – simply because, for example, those subject to a particular type of control do not question its legitimacy or can see no alternative'.[10]

The development and maintenance of legitimacy is expressed in a variety of ideological statements, which defend and justify the exercise of power by elites in, for example, the military and the police, the church and the trade unions, the civil service and the universities. Occupational ideologies are a special case which seek to legitimise the power and special status of such groups as doctors or solicitors, skilled craftsmen or others who exercise, through their occupation, power over others within their employing organisation or within society at large.

The development of industrial and commercial enterprise has been marked by shifts both in the distribution and the basis of power. A significant change has occurred with the growth of share-holdings and on the one hand their fragmentation and dispersal and on the other their concentration among institutional holders. Both these trends have added to the power of internal company management and, it might be argued, have made it more difficult to locate exactly the locus of decision-making. Top level strategic decisions may now be made not by a few major shareholders or even at board level, but among senior management advisors to the board. Just as shareholders have become more remote from their companies, so too, developments in company structure – the growth of multinationals, of holding companies or of heavily diversified organisations – have rendered decision-making power still more remote and unapproachable both to workers and to local management.

We should not overstate the power of senior management, however, as an independent force. There is considerable affinity of interest between management and shareholders and the fragmentation and institutionalisation of shareholdings may have increased the power of large minority shareholders or executive directors.[11]

Such changes in the structure of much of private industrial and commercial enterprise and associated changes in the bases of power in such organisations have been matched by changes in ideology. Management is less likely to justify its exercise of power on the grounds that it represents the interests of ownership and may appeal for legitimacy in terms of its expertise.[12] The growing distrust of experts referred to in the introduction, and of forms of 'elitism' in general may now be producing a new form of legitimacy based on shared decisions and the involvement of all affected parties in decision processes.

Closely linked with any discussion of power and authority is the question of conflict. Power relationships will be to varying degrees conflictual. An important element in subordinates' granting of legitimacy to the power of superiors will be the degree of consensus that exists over organisational objectives, values, norms and roles.

Writers on management and industrial relations have, over the years, taken quite different views of the nature and extent of conflict in organisations. At one extreme, organisations have been viewed as essentially *harmonic* with a large measure of agreement between various parties about the exercise of power and authority.[13] Such conflicts that exist, argues this school, are the result of such things as personality differences, poor communications or poor organisational design. Conflict is not inherent in organisations and is capable of being smoothed by appropriate organisational action.

A different perspective is that which may be described as *pluralist*.[14] Conflict is seen here as an inevitable part of organisational life. Given its inevitability, the task of management is not to remove the conflict but to accommodate it. The pluralist view of organisation is of different parties with different interests coming together to pursue these interests within a common organisational framework. The pursuit of a variety of interests necessarily leads to dispute over such items as the distribution of rewards, the allocation of work tasks and the establishment of major strategic as well as lesser tactical objectives.

In this pluralistic view of organisations, much unilateral power is not readily legitimised and cannot be successfully maintained over the long-term. Rather it is necessary for the various parties to bargain for an acceptance of their wishes. To facilitate such bargaining, interest groups will individually or collectively present their demands, and the resulting outcome will be one of compromise.

However, we should note that not all managerial power is opposed by workers in the pluralist conception. Rather there will be a range of subjects over which management is in practice viewed as having undisputed authority or as having to submit to the bargaining exercise.

A further group of writers have provided a critique of the pluralist position which leads to what we may call a *radical* perspective on industrial relations.[15] In this view, the pluralist conception is castigated as unrealistic in many of its assumptions. Bargaining, it is suggested, inevitably takes place between unequal parties because one party, management, has at its disposal large amounts of power, including the power of the state which, in the final resort, is committed to the support of property and the rights deriving from property. Management represents the *status quo* which the state will act to defend.

In this view of industrial relations, there is little point in pursuing any policy which will lead to the greater legitimacy of managerial power. At its extreme, the exercise of collective bargaining is seen as supportive of the unsatisfactory pluralist system. Collective bargaining provides a means of accommodation and continuation rather than revolution and the reconstruction of new forms of social relationships and new bases of power. Collective bargaining, it is argued, implicitly accepts the power of management, and provides it with legitimacy in certain areas in exchange for negotiating rights in others.

These alternative perspectives on the nature of both power and conflict may be seen to be associated with distinctive views of participation. Any discussion of participation is bedevilled by the number and range of terms used to describe participative methods. Attached to each are subtly different shades of meaning and one cannot regard the various terms as synonymous.

Some of the terms currently in use and which illustrate this point include, for example, workers' control, industrial democracy, self-management and participative management. Other terms current in this general area include job-enrichment, job-enlargement, management by agreement or, more remotely, management by objectives. More highly structured forms of participative practice include joint consultation, works councils and committees, co-ownership, co-partnership and worker directors.

How far are these simply alternative facets of the same central idea? How do they variously relate to each other and what fundamental themes are being tapped? It is not our intention in this book to offer definitions of this welter of alternative terms and titles or to seek to establish a fine discrimination between them. Nevertheless, the implementation of participation does demand that the parties involved clearly understand what they are about and the nature of the programme upon which they have embarked. It is necessary to appreciate the subtle differences that exist between the various terms and the alternative philosophies underlying different forms of participation.

The relationship between organisational philosophy and one's advocacy of one scheme of participation or another, can be readily illustrated. Proponents of the harmonic view of organisations, for example, have little need of participative schemes which recognise alternative sources of loyalty or power, or which seek to give alternative form to the expression of conflict. Schemes of joint consultation, the conferring of rights to information or possibly the development of work group autonomy would be congruent with the harmonic philosophy for as long as these schemes did not materially change management's prerogatives. As we shall see below, a major criticism of joint consultation and similar schemes has been their lack of real power to affect managerial decision-making.

At the other extreme, those holding what we have described as a radical view of industrial relations could be expected to reject any scheme of participation which lent support to and buttressed the institutions of capitalism. The only form of participation which is consistent with such a radical view is that which allows the development of worker control or schemes of self-management. As Topham has noted,

'In the field of industrial democracy ... there is always

a dividing line between reforms which genuinely advance workers' rights and those which achieve the incorporation of workers and the separation of the representatives from their constituents. The line is not fixed at the same point in all circumstances or historical periods, and we can learn from experience to be more clear as to where it does, in practice, lie in present circumstances. Moreover, the same institution – a works council, or a production committee – can be absorbed without threat to capitalism's preorogatives at one time, whilst proving a real extension of workers' rights at another.'[16]

Schemes of worker control and self-management go beyond merely weakening the power of capital to replacing it with entirely different power structures, based not on the investment of capital but the investment of labour. Such self-management objectives, if they were to be introduced on a wide scale would require not only changes within the organisation, but in the wider society also: a change, not only in the basis of authority at work but in the entire fabric of social relationships in our society and their economic and legal foundations. Thomason has referred to these views, as espousing a 'replacement' ideology, 'supporting a replacement of the owners as the power elite by a worker or worker-plus-state elite'.[17]

Participation, however, is consistent with a pluralist view of organisations. Such a view is not simply to do with the elimination of any one party but with moves to equalise the power of different parties. Such a conception is contradictory to the radical view and quite meaningless given a unitary, harmonic conception.

In this connection it is worth repeating the emphasis placed on *influence* rather than control in our introduction to this chapter. Given a pluralist perspective, participation becomes a question of sharing power rather than taking power. But the radical analysis is correct when it notes that sharing power must lead to sharing responsibility. Participation in a pluralist context, therefore, leads through a sharing of power and responsibility to new kinds of relationships between participants.

As it is this pluralist conception with which we as authors most closely identify, we will elaborate more fully on what we understand by such a perspective.

Following as they did chronologically upon the harmonic emphasis of 'human relations' thinking, writers who have taken a pluralist view have perhaps over-reacted to such ideas by stressing the conflictual basis of pluralism. While we agree with the pluralist view that conflict is endemic in complex organisations, it is worth noting in this respect that pluralism also implies subjects over which there is consensus and shared values. This is the position that Fox describes when he notes that

> 'it may be useful to consider degrees of commitment *to* management rule as being on a common scale with degrees of commitment *against* it. This would give us a continuum ranging from total acceptance of authority at one end to total rejection at the other.'[18]

Fox goes on to suggest that most situations will be somewhere between these two polar extremes.

Thus an important, though frequently over-looked, feature of pluralism which distinguishes it from the purely harmonic and the extreme radical perspectives is that both conflict and consensus are endemic in complex organisations. Fox had made this point earlier in his research paper for the Royal Commission on Trade Unions and Employers' Associations (hereafter the Donovan Committee). He writes,

> 'The full acceptance of the notion that an industrial organisation is made up of sectional groups with

divergent interests involves also a full acceptance of the fact that the degree of common purpose which can exist in industry is only of a very limited nature. In the sense that the groups are mutually dependent, they may be said to have a common interest in the survival of the whole of which they are parts. But this is essentially a remote long-term consideration which enters little into the day-to-day conduct of the organisation and cannot provide that harmony of operational objectives and methods for which managers naturally yearn.'[19]

The principle that consensus and conflict co-exist in organisations is recognised here as a feature of the pluralistic perspective. It may be that in special circumstances – for example in smaller firms, in one industry communities or at times of high unemployment – the 'common interest in survival' will be far from being a 'remote consideration'. It may be argued that in some circumstances this common interest is a feature of everyday life which gives both management and workers a common objective and provides a focus for consensus.

The focus of consensus, however, need not necessarily be restricted to the problem of survival. It is our experience across a number of industries that consensus exists about a range of management and worker prerogatives. The expectations that workers have of management's right to exercise power are derived from the education system, from newspapers and television, from novels and films. Much of the material developed through the media presents as if it were a natural fact, managers and workers, superiors and subordinates, playing distinctive roles. Put briefly, workers are socialised to accept both their role and the managerial role. Such socialisation in the wider society outside work, is a source of conformity and consensus within the employing organisation.

Furthermore, we should recognize that people work in

and are members of a range of complex organisations and are not simply employees in manufacturing industry. The organisations in which people live and work vary, for example in their size and structure, in their ownership, their history and their traditions. It is unrealistic to assume that there will be a common level of conflict in all these organisational settings or that there will be an absence of consensus universally. On the contrary, one might reasonably expect that there will be consensus over objectives, over the exercise of power and the distribution of rewards, in all organisations which continue to survive. Nor do we suggest that there will be or should be an absence of conflict in any of these situations, but simply that the amount of conflict that is found in an organisation will vary from situation to situation.

Furthermore, the subjects over which there is conflict or consensus will also vary from organisation to organisation. In some organisations, there may be consensus over ultimate values which continue to bind together the whole, despite conflict over details of day-to-day operation. In other organisations, a conflict over untimate values may be matched by agreement over day-to-day operational details. Churches, for example, illustrate the former situation, prisons the latter.

When one restricts the comparison to organisations concerned simply with industrial or commercial objectives, the range of variation will not be so great; but differences in the levels of conflict and consensus, and the subjects of conflict and consensus will continue to be found. Small and large organisations may be expected to vary in these respects. So too may organisations concerned with clerical rather than manual work, organisations with different ownership patterns, with different legacies of industrial relations tradition, with different technologies, markets, products, occupational groups or organisations existing in different parts of the country. It is beyond the scope of this book to examine in detail these many sources of variation. They lend weight, however, to our simple proposition that appreciation of the endemic nature of conflict must be matched by an appreciation of the endemic nature of consensus.

This is not to suggest a zero sum equation in which conflict and consensus will always mechanically balance. Rather, from situation to situation, the subjects of conflict and consensus will vary. It is thus possible in some organisations – for example, political parties, for there to be high levels of conflict and high levels of consensus. Elsewhere, in more apathetic organisations, low levels of both may be found. The amounts and subjects of conflict and consensus will also change over time.

If we accept this view of complex organisations as essentially pluralistic bodies with varying degrees of conflict and consensus, power and authority, it becomes possible to state more clearly the objectives that might be held for participation, and the means by which they may be pursued.

Because complex organisations are pluralist entities, industrial democracy is a meaningful concept. Because pluralist bodies contain elements of conflict *and* consensus, power *and* authority, participative schemes which permit an extension of democracy, can also pursue improvements in organisational effectiveness.

Participation and industrial democracy

A major difficulty with any evaluation of schemes of industrial democracy is the analogy that is made with the institutions of political democracy. Such analogies invariably dwell on such items as the arrangements for franchise, the drawing of constituencies or the number of 'seats' available. But there are obvious and significant differences between political and economic organisation, and particularly if participation is seen within a pluralistic context as a means of ensuring the coexistence of parties with very different interests in the organisation. Government 'of the people, by the people, for the people' may be a good basis for political democracy, but in the context of economic organisation it poses the questions 'who are the people?' and 'what are the boundaries of the organisation?' Does the organisation include only workers – or workers and management? Should it be extended to include shareholders – or shareholders and consumers? Should it include representatives of the community in which the enterprise is situated?

We shall note in later chapters the kind of constitutional arrangements that have been made for industrial democracy, but in these introductory comments we only wish to draw attention to what we regard as the fundamental underlying principle of any form of democratisation; this is a movement towards the equalisation of power. Whether the sharing of power should be in proportion to numbers, to investment, or at some agreed formula, be it 50–50, 49–51, $2X + Y$ or a token representation, is a political issue both for the wider society and, in the absence of legislation, for each individual company. The majority of the Committee of Inquiry on Industrial Democracy (the Bullock Committee) reported in favour of the extension of industrial democracy by legislating for the representation of organised labour on the boards of large companies. The formula which they recommended was $2X + Y$ – equal numbers of employee and shareholder representatives together with a number of neutral members.[20] This proposal has met with much criticism – and not only from the employer representatives on the Bullock Committee itself. The opposition to the Bullock proposals is instructive in terms of the discussion that we have undertaken in this chapter. Three main sources of criticism may be identified, though it should be recognised that it is difficult to know how much credence can be placed on public statements when they may simply be a rationalisation of private motivations. The first source of opposition has been from the representatives of employers. An obvious reason for their opposition can be seen in the dilution of power that is expected to accompany the implementation of the proposals. Employers' groups have also pointed to the dangers of lost efficiency and effectiveness that might occur if senior decision-making boards became arenas for pre-emptive collective bargaining. We shall return to the relationship of participation and efficiency below.

A second source of opposition has come from extreme socialist and communist groups who see collaboration with the institutions of capitalism as delaying rather than advancing the ultimate replacement of the system. The Communist Party of Great Britain, for example, in its evidence to Bullock noted

'as far as private industry is concerned .... We are completely opposed to the concept of Worker Directors and the Supervisory Board'.[21]

Such arrangements, it suggests, are 'a means of enmeshing the workers in the running of private industry based on production for profit'.[22] Communist groups in other Western countries have expressed similar views. Batstone, for example, reports that the CGT in France rejects similar forms of participation.[23]

In Britain the Communist Party saw collective bargaining as a major means of achieving industrial democracy. This is the position also of the third group from whom opposition to the Bullock proposals has come – parts of the trade union movement. Certain unions, although not seeking to destroy our existing pluralism, prefer to see its achievement through the institutions of collective bargaining rather than through formal representation on company boards. Such an approach to industrial democracy was most notably advocated by Clegg some twenty years ago. One of the main strengths of this approach lies in the *independent* power with which employees are able to challenge managerial prerogatives. Against this advantage, however, it is clear that such employee power derives only from collective strength requiring union organisation. Whatever form of industrial democracy is adopted, the need for trade unions will continue. But if the unions are the main vehicle for industrial democracy through collective bargaining, one must avoid the risk of replacing autocratic management with oligarchic trade unions. For collective bargaining to be a viable form of democracy, it is essential that democratic procedures are safeguarded within the trade unions themselves.

A further difficulty that has been noted in the collective bargaining approach to industrial democracy is that while trade unions can provide effective opposition, they cannot provide an alternative government. It is possible to have a viable democracy in which one group remains in *permanent* opposition? However we should bear in mind the danger referred to above of making too ready an analogy with political democracy, and ask rather how far collective bargaining has entailed a sharing of power and the responsibilities that go with that share of power.

One main criticism that we would make of the Bullock report lies not so much with the report itself as with its terms of reference, which limited its considerations to representation on boards of directors. Quite apart from the questions that must be asked about the extent to which formal meetings of boards of directors are the locus of power, such a narrow preoccupation avoids consideration of the way decision-making power is exercised at every level throughout the organisation.

Figure 1.1   Participation and Decision Hierarchies

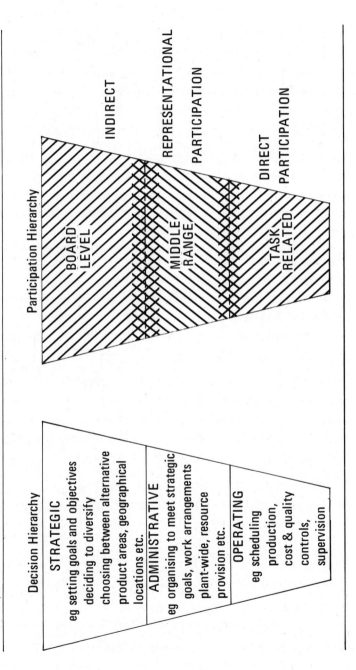

Organisational decision-making may be seen as a hierarchy, shaped like an inverted pyramid. At the top lie the wide-ranging strategic decisions with a broad sweep of implications for people operating throughout the organisation. They are followed by a middle range of decision-making of more limited application which is required to organise for the implementation of the strategic decisions. This in turn is followed by still narrower decisions down to the level of the individual task.*

Such a simple three-fold classification runs the risk of over-simplifying the structure of decisions. Some writers have produced more complex descriptions but the categories described above adequately illustrate the concept of a hierarchy of decision-making with which truly effective schemes of participation need to come to terms.

The extension of participation – a growth in the ability to influence decisions by sharing decision-making power – may thus be located at any of the levels we have described. Schemes of participation may be readily found which concentrate on one of these levels. One can point, for example, to job enrichment schemes which share the power to make task-related decisions, or to works committees which share power over certain middle range decisions. However, the various kinds of decision-making described by the hierarchy in Figure 1.1 are interdependent. Strategic, top-level decisions limit the possibilities for middle-range and for operating decisions. They also determine the areas in which such lower levels of decision-making need to occur.

---

*This simplified hierarchy of decision-making is based on the ideas of Igor Ansoff as presented, for example. in *Corporate Strategy* McGraw-Hill (New York, 1965). At the lower levels, however, we would extend participation below his 'operating decisions' to include decisions which are so closely related to the primary work task as to be hardly managerial in content at all. Also, the boundaries of our board level, middle-range and task related decisions are not exact overlaps with the strategic, administrative and operating decisions.

For this reason, participation which is confined to the lower levels of decision-making may appear a sham. Because of the limitations imposed by the higher level decisions, the restricted range of alternatives left to the lower level participants may cause more disaffection than openly autocratic management.

But strategic decisions require information from all parts of the organisation. Board level participation without a similar involvement at lower levels will reduce the effectiveness of the board representatives in obtaining and using accurate information for strategic decision.

Participation in middle-range and operating decisions will be regarded cynically if unilateral strategic decisions continually frustrate and render useless such participative effort. Participation at board level will be a paper exercise if it is not followed through by greater levels of involvement at middle-range and operational levels of decision.

A major theme of this book is that the extension of participation, if undertaken at all, should be undertaken as an integrated organisation-wide activity. Participation is about sharing power and therefore sharing responsibility; this cannot be isolated in one department or at one hierarchical level.

Conclusion

In this chapter we have discussed alternative perspectives on participation and on organisational relationships more generally. We have concluded that participation is about sharing influence over decisions and that this occurs in organisations which are essentially pluralist. Although pluralist organisations are well placed so to extend participation, we cannot assume that the parties involved will be immediately enthusiastic. Managers may be reluctant to be involved in what they perceive as a dilution of their power. Workers may be reluctant to accept what they perceive as an essentially managerial responsibility.

In as much as participation is a sharing of power, it is a basic form of democratisation. But participation may be introduced for reasons other than a wish to see democracy extended. Some may wish to see an improvement in the quality of working life by enlarging jobs to include a greater amount of decision-making. This may be done for moral or humanitarian reasons or it may be believed that such job re-design will lead to greater productivity or to lower labour turnover or absenteeism. Similarly, schemes to extend participation at other levels in the organisation may be designed to improve organisational effectiveness by improving the quality of decision-making and the levels of involvement rather than for democratic purposes *per se*. In a pluralistic organisation one would expect such a plurality of motivation over any matter of policy.

We have suggested that all schemes of participation which result in some sharing of power represent a basic democratisation. To avoid confusion, however, we shall from here on reserve the term 'industrial democracy' to refer to those schemes of participation which explicitly seek power sharing for its own sake. As we have noted, such schemes usually seek to parallel political forms. They may be contrasted with the use of participation for the other objectives referred to above. In considering the forms that participation may take and the criteria to be used in its evaluation, these distinctions between alternative objectives are crucial.

A note of caution should be sounded, however. There is no necessary relationship between the continued extension of industrial democracy and, for example, improved organisational performance. There may even be conflict between forms of participation which optimise one objective at the expense of another.

There are no ideal or universally applicable schemes of participation. The purpose of this book is to point to the variability of such schemes and to the variability of the organisational contexts in which they must operate. The extension of participation will not just happen – it must be made to happen. The development of participation is thus a managerial task (but not, we emphasise, a task for the management group alone). It is a task that needs to be managed in that it needs objectives and policy, methods and programmes, evaluation and review. The group responsible for participation should be aware of the alternatives before them – and of the organisational context in which participation must occur. Most importantly, however, those responsible for the extension of participation should be aware of the social changes upon which they are embarking. To repeat the point we made in the introduction to this chapter, participation involves changed attitudes and expectations. Participation will be associated with new kinds of relationships based on trust rather than on formal contract. In building such relationships the organisation is embarking on an irreversible process. For this reason it is essential that organisations handle the subject with careful forethought and delicacy and that there is commitment from the top-most levels.

We return in later chapters to the implementation of participation. In the next three chapter, however, we shall examine alternative forms of participation in different countries and with different objectives.

References

1. J. Wellens, *Worker Participation: A Practical Policy,* Wellens Publishing (Guilsborough 1975), p. 3.
2. A. Fox, *Man Mismanagement*, Hutchinson (London 1974), pp.94–6.
3. D. Guest and D. Fatchett, *Worker Participation: Individual Control and Performance*, (London 1974), p. 10.

4. *Ibid.*, p.11.
5. A.S. Tannenbaum, *Social Psychology of the Work Organisation,* Tavistock (London 1973), p. 85.
6. *Ibid.*, p.84.
7. A.S. Tannenbaum, *Control in Organisations,* McGraw-Hill (New York 1968), p. 5.
8. M. Poole, *Workers' Participation in Industry,* Routledge and Kegan Paul (London 1975), p.26.
9. J.R.P. French, J. Israel and D. Äs, 'An Experiment on Participation in a Norwegian Factory' *Human Relations* Vol. 13, (1960), pp. 3–19.
10. R. Hyman, *Industrial Relations: A Marxist Introduction,* Macmillan (London 1975), p. 26.
11. For detailed discussion of these ideas see J. Child, *British Management Thought,* Allen and Unwin (London 1969), and T. Nichols, *Ownership, Control and Ideology,* Allen and Unwin (London 1969).
12. R. Bendix, *Work and Authority in Industry,* Wiley (New York 1956).
13. An example of this view is provided by G.C. Homans, 'Some Corrections to "The Perspectives of Elton Mayo"', *Review of Economics and Statistics,* Vol. 31, (1949), pp. 319–21.
14. R. Bendix and L.H. Fisher, 'The Perspectives of Elton Mayo', *Review of Economics and Statistics,* Vol 31, (1949), pp. 312–19. See also A. Fox, *Industrial Sociology and Industrial Relations,* Royal Commission on Trade Unions and Employers' Associations, Research Paper No. 3, HMSO (London 1966).
15. See A. Fox, 'Industrial Relations: A Social Critique of Pluralist Ideology', in J. Child (Ed.), *Man and Organisation: The Search for Explanation and Social Relevance,* Allen and Unwin (London 1973).
16. A. Topham, 'A Four Point Policy for the Unions' *Tribune,* 25 February 1966.
17. G.F. Thomason, 'Workers' Participation in Private

Enterprise Organisations', in Campbell Balfour, *Participation in Industry*, Croom Helm (London 1973), p. 139.

18. A. Fox, *A Sociology of Work in Industry*, Collier-Macmillan (London 1971), p. 44.

19. A. Fox, *Industrial Sociology and Industrial Relations, op. cit.*, p. 4.

20. *Report of the Committee of Inquiry on Industrial Democracy*, HMSO (London 1977). A precedent for this formula may be found in the proposals for worker representation on the board of Harland and Wolff. (See *The Financial Times* 19 August, 1975, 'Worker Participation to keep the Wolf from Harland's Door'.) On this occasion, however, the proposal was for a two-tier board.

21. The Communist Party of Great Britain, *Evidence to the Committee of Inquiry on Industrial Democracy*, (London 1976), pp. 4–5.

22. *Ibid*, p. 5.

23. E. Batstone, 'Industrial Democracy and Worker Representation at Board Level: A Review of European Experience', in E. Batstone and P.L. Davies, *Industrial Democracy: European Experience*, HMSO (London 1976).

2 Participation at board level

Introduction

The most dramatic form of indirect participation is probably the appointment of worker representatives to the boards of directors of companies. It is doubtful, however, whether it is also the most effective means of securing participation.

Worker directorships extend participation in terms of our definition by permitting a greater range of people to exert influence over organisational decision-making. Representation at board level is a form of power sharing and a ready means of obtaining an extension of industrial democracy.

It should not be assumed, however, that the extension of industrial democracy is the only objective that is held for worker directorships. It is true that for many groups the extension of industrial democracy is an end in itself requiring no further justification. Such groups are unlikely to be satisfied with just *any* form of power sharing that may be offered but, as we suggested in the last chapter, may well have aspirations based on their experience of political democracy. For others, however, the power sharing inherent in any form of participation will be incidental to other objectives. The most obvious example of this position is the pursuit through limited worker involvement at board level of improved organisational effectiveness.

The pursuit of representation for democratic objectives

alone will not necessarily be compatible with effectiveness objectives. Democratic objectives will seek ultimately equality of representation for distinctive interest groups – effectiveness objectives will concentrate rather on the *contribution* that different groups can make. Democratic objectives will make necessary, for example, appropriate election procedures and the representation of different interests by drawing up constituencies. Effectiveness objectives may seek appointment on some basis other than electoral popularity such as, for example, expertise in a particular area. They will emphasise not representation but identification with board membership and board objectives. They may require a level of confidentiality which places constraints on reporting back to constituents.

In Britain, experience of worker directors has been sparse. In this chapter we shall examine forms of involvement in strategic decision-making in both private and nationalised companies which have sought to enhance either the sharing of power for its own sake or for the more effective pursuit of organisational objectives. We shall then examine an example of the European experience of worker directors.

Worker directorships and co-ownership

One answer to the problems raised by the conflicting interests of shareholders and employees has been to merge the two groups. Several examples of the policy of 'economic democracy' may be found of which a leading UK example is the Scott Bader Company. Schumacher, one of the original trustees of the company, has described its approach to reconciling the interests of owners and employees as 'effecting the *extinction* of private ownership rather than as the establishment of collective ownership'.[1] This was initiated in 1951 when Ernest Bader, founder of the company, gave ninety per cent of his holding to the employees by the establishment of a commonwealth. The process was completed twelve years later when the remaining ten per cent of shares were re-distributed. The company, currently employing some 350–400 employees, operates through a Commonwealth (the total body of company employees), and a Community Council consisting of fifteen members elected by fifteen constituencies which have power to approve or disapprove the Chairman's appointees to the Board of Directors and their remuneration. The Community Council receives reports from the Directors and is the final arbiter in any dispute. The Board of Directors contains executive and non-executive directors and acts in a conventional manner apart only from the distinctive nature of its appointment and accountability. Finally a body of seven Trustees is appointed by the Community Council (two members), the Board of Directors (two members) and the two acting jointly (three members). The tasks of the Trustees are to safeguard the constitution of the Company and prevent either the Community Council or the Board of Directors from acting in breach of it; secondly they arbitrate between the Community Council and the Board of Directors in the event of deadlock in matters of basic policy; finally they are called upon to act should the company begin running at a loss.

While the Company has continued with commercial success, several distinctive features should be noted. Perhaps most important is that the Company is not totally committed to economic objectives. The redistribution of shareholdings, for example, had a religious rather than a commercial origin. In a preamble to the Company's constitution it is stated that 'far-reaching reconstruction cannot be delayed and …. the principle of Common-ownership in industry, based on the requirements of a peaceful society, represent essential steps towards a true Christian Industrial and Social Order'.[2] In a similar vein the Company eschews participation in the production of any product which has an application in war. The Company declares as one of its objectives in its Memorandum and Articles of Association, 'to contribute towards the general welfare of society, internationally, nationally and in the company's immediate neighbourhood'.[3]

A further and obvious feature is the total realisation of capital. The distinction between capital and labour is totally abandoned and all participants are seen as colleagues. Although members are free to join trade unions, there is a total commitment to the search for equitable remuneration within the firm and very high levels of job security. The Company's Code of Practice, adopted in 1972 declares that,

> 'in the event of a down-turn in trade we will share all the remaining work rather than expect any of our fellow-members to be deprived of employment, even if this requires a reduction in earnings by all'.[4]

Without more focussed research it is not possible to distinguish the amount of success that may be due to the Commonwealth form of organisation from that which flows from other factors. There are few other companies to which one can turn for comparison. Kalamazoo embarked on a similar project but by incremental stages which have now been halted by legal technicalities connected with the death of the founder.[5] The case of Ford, Ayrton and Company, described by Thomason, demonstrates that participation alone cannot save a company in the face of disastrously adverse market conditions.[6] In circumstances of increased foreign competition, the firm closed after some fifty years of co-partnership. The more recent experience of the Scottish Daily News co-operative also suggests that a participative form of organisation does not allow a company to avoid the realities of the economic environment. It is possible that the Scott Bader success is due, at least in part, to a favourable market situation which a small and successfully participative organisation has been well placed to exploit. This is not to detract from the Scott Bader record but rather to point to the circumstances within which it has occurred.

Perhaps the best known form of industrial democracy in Britain is the John Lewis Partnership. This Partnership shares a number of similar institutional forms to the Scott Bader Company. There is a Chairman, a Constitution and a body of Trustees. There is also a Board of Directors (The Central Board), a Central Council (with several sub-committees), a series of Branch Councils, Committees for Communication (an open forum for rank and file discussion at branch level) and a number of Registrars.

These institutions form two quite different strands – the executive and the representative – with the Chairman at the head of each. The representative strand has direct responsibilities for welfare and expenditure on some other limited items. The executive strand comprising the Chairman, Board of Directors and management hierarchy is responsible for the Company's business strategy and its implementation. The exception to this division lies in the ultimate, if somewhat qualified, power of the Central Council to remove the Chairman from office.

This is achieved by a simple 'Resolution upon the Constitution' passed by a two-thirds majority and implemented by the Trustees. The voting shares of the Company are divided between the Chairman and the Trustees in the ratio 41:60, but the Trustees' voting power is reserved for removing the Chairman following a Central Council resolution. The Trustees, who are appointed by the Central Council, then have the responsibility to appoint a new Chairman and this gives them the option to re-appoint the sacked Chairman.

To date, this procedure has proved academic as it has never been invoked. The activities of the representative strand *vis-à-vis* executive action has been limited to providing a feedback of opinion and receiving information.

Figure 2.1 The Institutions of the John Lewis Partnership

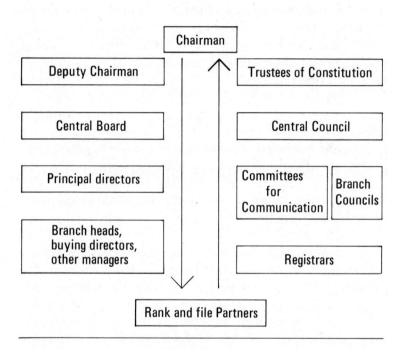

As Flanders and his colleagues noted in their examination of the Partnership published in 1968, 'in this respect they are no more than the equivalent of machinery for consultation'.[7] The Central and Branch Councils, they add, are 'in fact – though it need not be so in theory – more representative of management than of the rank and file'.[8] The Committees of Communication are entirely rank and file with the exception of their chairmen but their main functions are to 'enquire, discuss and suggest'. They can thus draw management's attention to problems and grievances but they cannot directly take action to correct these problems.

The executive strand headed by the Chairman and the

Board of Directors operates on the principle of management accountability rather than direct control from the representative structure. The Board of Directors is partly nominated by the Central Council but only in minority terms. Of twelve directors, five are nominated by the Central Council and seven by the Chairman including the Chairman himself and his Deputy. The theoretical safeguard that remains is the power of the Central Council to remove the Chairman.

Finally it should be noted that the Partnership operates a substantial profit-sharing scheme. After meeting proper claims and holding a reserve for future development, all profits are distributed in proportion to pay. In 1973–74 nearly £4 million were distributed at the rate of fifteen per cent of annual salary. In the same year £11 million was retained for further development or other employee benefits.

The John Lewis and Scott Bader organisations provide an interesting comparison. An obvious difference lies in the respective size of the two organisations. At Scott Bader with some 370 employees it is possible for the Chairman personally to address all members of the organisation at a single plenary session and to receive questions and enter into a meaningful interaction. At John Lewis, with an organisational membership of between 22,000 and 23,000 no such direct interaction is possible and it is perhaps inevitable that the participation will take a more bureauratic form in the sense that formal institutions will have clear rights and duties and boundaries to their authority. Given such a structure moreover, and given the essentially advisory role of the representative bodies, it is perhaps inevitable that shop-floor involvement in the scheme might be at a low level. Flanders and his colleagues found that among rank and file employees with no special status or responsibility within the representative structure, there were considerable divisions between groups of employees in the levels of interest evidenced.[9] Table 2.1 gives a break-down of these figures and shows that overall some sixty-one per cent of such employees may be regarded as having a 'lower interest' – i.e. readership of the Partnership's publications on the democratic experiments and results of a test on knowledge about the democratic institutions.

Both companies, it should be noted, have a distinctive occupational structure. John Lewis is largely involved in white collar employment while twenty per cent of Scott Bader employees work in laboratories and the depersonalising assembly line situation is absent. We shall discuss in Chapter 5 the implications of factors such as these for successful participation. In the remainder of this chapter, we will examine forms of participation in quite different conditions of size and technology.

Table 2.1 Democratic interest in the John Lewis Partnership by sex and length of service among employees with no special status or responsibility

	Lower interest	Higher interest	Totals
Men			
1–5 years' service	75	41	116
5 + years' service	43	38	81
Women			
1–5 years' service	95	34	129
5 + years' service	38	48	86
Totals	251	161	412

A. Flanders, R. Pomeranz, and J. Woodward, *Experiment in Industrial Democracy*, Faber and Faber (London, 1968), Table 13, p. 86.

Worker directorships for greater effectiveness

The first British company to adopt a two-tier board structure to enable the appointment of worker directors was Bonser Engineering Limited. Its Memorandum and Articles of Association were amended in this way in 1976.

The Bonser development is largely the brain-child of its chief executive, Carl Duerr. Duerr has a substantial record in Britain and elsewhere in Europe as a management consultant specialising in the rescue of 'ailing' companies.

The Bonser company had been a successful manufacturer of pit-props in Nottinghamshire until, with the decline of the coal industry in the 1960s, it was obliged to sell its interest in this activity. The company thereafter developed its expertise in hydraulics by the manufacture of fork-lift trucks – an activity it was already involved with in a small way. Despite a large demand for the new product, the company found it difficult to adapt to its new circumstances. The death of the chairman and the ensuing succession crisis finally brought about the situation in which Duerr was invited to be consultant and ultimately chief executive.

The operation of the worker director scheme at Bonser clearly owes a great deal to the charisma and dynamism of Duerr himself. On joining the company, he set about implementing his management philosophy as set out in his book *Management Kinetics*.[10] At the heart of this philosophy is a belief in the overlapping interests of shareholders and all those who work for the company. This leads to the major themes in his management style – the need for good communications, the need to develop high levels of trust and confidence between all groups involved in the company, and the need for a high level of 'professionalism' in all the jobs that need to be completed.

The company is small enough to allow face to face communications between Duerr and all the employees. He regularly walks around the plant talking to employees about their personal or work problems. He regularly addresses all employees in plenary sessions. The company has grown by acquiring similarly sized outfits where managing directors are encouraged to adopt a similar style.

The size of the company, Duerr's personal knowledge of the workers and his dynamism and overt commitment to the company's success – he is regularly at work ahead of the factory – have helped rapidly to establish a bond of trust within the plant. Duerr believes that such trust is a natural concomitant of full and open communications. It has also been helped by Duerr's preparedness to use trade union channels and to avoid using his communication style to by-pass or out-box the trade unions.

But it is perhaps his belief in professionalism that has most strongly influenced his approach to worker directors. He notes in his own forthright style,

> 'we don't want the jig borer or the computer operator mucking about with the specialities of line management. Not unless he gets himself a lot of specialised training and education. And we don't want the line manager fooling around with a £50,000 Swiss jig borer or a £100,000 computer programme. Not unless he's similarly educated in the speciality. But given the right personal qualifications, with perhaps a bit of crash-training in accounts and company law, any of them could well make good supervisory board members – the people who watch from above and monitor the performance of management. And have the authoritative control over management.'[11]

Worker directors in Bonser will be selected and appointed for their knowledge of the shop floor and the contribution that this allows them to make to the quality of the supervisory board's decisions. Directors are not on the board at Bonser to represent sectional interests; they represent specialist experience. It is this concern with the contribution that specialist knowledge can make that has led Duerr to separate the 'Governing Board's' function clearly from those of the 'Executive Board'.

The Governing Board is concerned with

'the determination of Company policy, the co-ordination of that policy with the Executive Board, the assessment and approval of consolidated Company budgets, targets and plans, and the monitoring and disciplining of executive performance accordingly'.[12]

The Executive Board is appointed by the Governing Board and is responsible for 'the day-to-day management of the Company in accordance with the policy of the Governing Board'.[13]

Duerr's influence on company performance to date has undoubtedly been beneficial. Duerr found a company earning most of its profits from interest on investments, with no basic management system and with low morale and high labour turnover. Prior to Duerr's arrival there had been a $62^1/_2$ per cent labour turnover in one period of six months. Duerr's record has been impressive in reversing these trends. Production quadrupled between 1972 and 1975. Profits have increased by almost the same amount – but a much higher proportion is now a trading profit. Labour turnover is no longer a problem.

But this is only partly due to increased participation. New management systems have been introduced. Wages have been brought into line with local rates of pay. Prices have been increased where it was recognised they were lagging behind their competitors, and, perhaps most importantly, subsidiary companies have been acquired and they now contribute to the total company record.

Furthermore, the record of improvement pre-dates the

constitutional changes in the articles of association which were ratified in April 1976.

However there is no doubt in the minds of the authors that Bonser's improved performance is in no small way due to the personal participative style of Duerr himself. The questions that remain to be answered are how far this style could continue in the absence of Duerr, and how far he would himself have succeeded in, for example, a large company or a company with a tradition of militant industrial relations. Duerr believes that his style is applicable in larger companies. The time taken to establish trust might be longer and the machinery used might be different. He suggests, furthermore, that his participative management style is being adopted by managing directors in the subsidiary companies and that he will gradually work himself out of his job.

In this situation, the worker director is a part of a total company philosophy on participation. This is a particularly coherent philosophy being the product of one man's long consideration of the matter. It is not designed as an extension of democracy but, on the contrary, adopts explicitly managerialist practices to obtain its ends. It concentrates attention, not on the special interests of particular groups, but on the contribution to the whole. It has been accompanied by increasing commercial success which has allowed various groups to meet their objectives within the overall consensus. Apart from the importance of one charismatic leader in this situation, we might question how far participation for improved effectiveness could survive a sustained period of falling profits and contraction.

Worker directorships at the British Steel Corporation

In contrast to the above, a further example of indirect participation through the mechanism of worker representation on boards of directors is to be found in the

British nationalised industries and most particularly in the British Steel Corporation. The establishment by the Attlee administration of the major nationalised industries provided not only an opportunity but an obligation upon the Labour Government to ensure representation of the workers' interests at Board level. This opportunity, however, brought with it its own problems, and in particular the determination of the relationship which was to hold between worker (in practice, trade union) representatives, and the workers in a particular industry, their trade unions, the management, the political overlords and that intangible thing, the organisation itself. Put crudely, were trade unionists on the nationalised boards to remain primarily union men carrying the union interests and the negotiation style into board's discussions or did they owe a primary loyalty to the industry as a whole – albeit a loyalty which they pursued with a distinctive orientation arising from their background and experience? The Labour Party had already faced this problem with the London Passenger Transport Bill of 1932. The reality of this practical situation demonstrated clearly the alternatives. Was there to be direct trade union participation in the control of the new organisation as demanded by the Transport and General Workers Union, or was control to be exercised through political institutions with boards of particular industries selected primarily for their ability to contribute to the efficient operation of the industry? In 1932 the TUC supported the Government in the latter policy and although subsequently adopting the opposite position, the TUC and the Labour Party also took this line during the critical years of the 1940s when the organisation of the new nationalised boards was being determined.

The position adopted on the London Passenger Transport Bill (and the subsequent nationalisation of the 1940s) was justified by Herbert Morrison.

'I want (working-class people) to be appointed on grounds of personal capacity; .... I want them to sit at the Board table, not as workmen guaranteed seats by an Act of Parliamentary charity, but as full equals, appointed by a Minister of the Crown, because of their personal fitness for the duties to be discharged.'[14]

This re-stated the position he had adopted at the 1932 Labour Party conference when he also emphasised that Board appointments should be on the grounds of ability. In his speech to that conference he distinguished between syndicalists, with their demands for workers' control, and Socialists for whom, he said, Board appointments should be based on 'individual capacity'.

'I beg you not to move from that point – that the final test of appointment shall be individual capacity ...'[15]

The traditional composition of boards of nationalised industries in Britain has subsequently been based primarily on ability rather than representation of (and reporting back to) sectional interests. In judging this criterion it has been recognised that labour and trade unions as well as former owners and managers have much to contribute to the successful operation of the industry. But when trade unionists have been appointed, they have been expected to sever their union affiliation and have acted in their own right as board members.

It was essentially a continuation of this debate that led to the decision to experiment further with workers' representation at board level in the new British Steel Corporation in 1968. The motives of the different parties involved in deciding to proceed with the worker directors scheme will probably never be fully known, though Brannen and his colleagues explore the matter in some

detail in their evaluative report on the project.[16] They point
to proposals made by the National Craftsmen's Co-
ordinating Committee and the Institute for Workers'
Control. They also draw attention to the way in which the
organising committee for the Steel Corporation sought to
maintain the initiative on the issue of participation by
producing proposals of its own in the light of the comments
of a variety of bodies. Important in this process was the
mixture of individuals concerned, both on the committee
and in government. Lord Melchett, the chairman designate
of the board, and Ron Smith, board member responsible
for personnel and industrial relations and a former general
secretary of the Union of Post Office Workers, were key
members of the organising committee with some pre-
disposition to participation. Brannen *et al* suggest that they
were encouraged in their experimental ideas by the attitude
of the Minister in charge, Richard Marsh.

On the other hand, as subsequent members were
appointed to the committee, total commitment to the idea
of worker participation became more tentative and
alternative opinions made themselves heard. Furthermore,
it became clear that trade union support was not
unanimous and indeed one major union, the electricians,
has not participated in the eventual scheme that was
implemented. Other unions varied from the view that
worker participation did not go far enough, to a defensive
sensitivity to the implied criticism that the scheme held for
its own efforts on behalf of its members.

Brannen and his colleagues suggest an outcome which re-
echoes much of Morrison's view of thirty-five years earlier.
That is that the eventual scheme was justified in terms of
'the organisational advantages likely to accrue'[17] and the
instrumental value of worker directors in bridging the gap
between policy making and the shop-floor.

The scheme itself originally involved the appointment of
three worker directors to each of the four group boards on
a part-time basis; for the remainder of the time they would

carry on with their normal jobs. The actual appointments were made by the chairman after a complex procedure involving trade unions and the TUC in the drawing up of a shortlist. As with earlier nationalisation, however, the appointees were required to relinquish their formal trade union posts.

As a result of this latter point, the underlying philosophy of the worker director experiment can hardly be said to be fundamentally different from the main tradition of labour involvement in nationalised industries' decision-making – apart, of course, from the unique position they hold in continuing their normal occupations.

Many of the difficulties encountered seem to have stemmed from the particular combination of traditional practice and innovatory thinking. Traditional practice meant that the members chosen became more distant from the union and even from the rank and file membership. They begin to be regarded as directors first and workers second. The experiment certainly did not alter trade union behaviour *vis-à-vis* the BSC or the divisional boards. The innovatory aspects, however, created difficulties. Retaining their normal jobs inevitably produced role tensions for management who were now placed in authority over their own directors. The constant need to be absent from work not only for meetings of the board but for training, for preparation, for travel created day-to-day problems for supervision and for men who had to cover for them during their absence.

Their contribution to the board meetings was similarly qualified. It should be recognised that the worker directors only sat at divisional board level and not at corporate level and that the function of the divisional boards was simply to offer advice. Divisional managing directors represented the focus of power at their level and it was up to these men to decide how they would use their divisional boards.

Within their advisory boards, the activities of the worker directors appear to have been further limited. The main topics on which they contributed were in the personnel and industrial relations areas yet these were relatively minor topics when viewed against the total range of subjects discussed by the boards. Brannen *et al* conclude that the worker directors spent thirty-four per cent of their time on twelve per cent of the boards' business.[18] In the contrary direction, a further weakness lay in the vague terms of reference given the worker directors. Other directors had very specialised knowledge and they could safely confine themselves to that. Worker directors spread themselves fairly evenly over most topic areas apart from personnel and industrial relations. Their main activity on the boards was to seek information rather than contribute positive suggestions. In instances where they did seek a more positive role Brannen and his colleagues suggest that the social system of the boards served to nullify their actions.

It must be recognised that it is still early days. The Brannen study covered only the first four years of the British Steel experiment. It would seem likely, however, that time will only result in a succession of worker directors learning anew the conflicts and tensions of the role. Although some experience may be passed on, the remainder of the board will have the better opportunity to contain the new men and structure their expectations of what they may legitimately do. All this, moreover, occurs within an institutional framework defining the role of the boards, limiting the worker directors' involvement with their trade unions and nurturing new relationships with board members. We return to some of these issues below.

Worker directorships and co-determination

Of the European experience, perhaps the most influential has been that of West Germany. As we shall see, it is dangerous to seize upon one part of any country's industrial machinery and seek to apply that elsewhere. In the case of West Germany the worker directors appointed as a result of the co-determination legislation, operate in a broader German industrial relations context. This involves a rationalised labour movement comprising only sixteen trade unions which negotiate legally enforceable and extendable collective bargains. It comprises also a tradition of works councils which pre-date the current legislation and have their origin in the Imperial Germany before 1914. It is into this specific industrial relations environment together with the broader cultural features of German society that the idea of co-determination was introduced by the occupying powers in 1948 and subsequently in Federal legislation for the coal, iron and steel industries in 1951.

German company law, furthermore, requires a two-tier board system in which a supervisory board is responsible for long-term business policy and appoints in turn a management board responsible for the day-to-day operation of the company. It is with the election and constitution of the supervisory board that co-determination legislation has been largely concerned.

The 1951 co-determination legislation, although limited in its effects to some half-million workers in the coal, iron and steel industries, will be described first because it lays down the basic model which subsequent legislation has followed and because it illustrates some of the main problems and issues associated with this method of obtaining worker representation on the boards of companies.

For most firms, the legislation required supervisory boards of eleven members.* Of these, four were to be appointed by shareholders and four by employees. Of the four employee representatives, two were to be nominated by the works council with the agreement of the trades unions and two were to be appointed by the trade unions centrally with the agreement of the works council. The two

---

*Larger firms were required to appoint fifteen or twenty-one members, but on the same basic principles as those described above.

works council nominees were to be respectively a wage-earner and a salaried employee. Two further representatives were to be appointed as 'independents'; one each by shareholders and employers respectively. These members were to be independent in that they were not to be members of a trade union or employers' association nor were they to be company employees or hold any other substantial financial interest in it. Thus both shareholders and employees contribute five members each to the board, one of whom on each side is an 'independent'. The most difficult clauses, however, surround the appointment of the so-called 'eleventh man' who clearly could hold the balance in the event of deadlock.

The legislation hedges this appointment about with all manner of safeguards and conditions. Although it was the intention of the Act that he should be a neutral person elected by the remainder of the supervisory board it has been necessary to frame with great care the conditions that surround his nomination and the nature of the majority on which his election must be based. In the final analysis, however, if the supervisory board fails to make an appointment, the task of appointing an eleventh man falls to the shareholders' general meeting. This has led some commentators to suggest that German co-determination in fact changes little as worker representatives are in a minority on the boards and although the legislation gives the appearance of parity, it must in the last resort, fall short of this.

A further significant part of the 1951 Act concerned the appointment to the lower tier board – the management board – of a personnel or labour director. His appointment or dismissal requires a majority of employee representatives on the supervisory board.

Further legislation in 1952 required employee representatives to one-third of supervisory boards of companies outside coal, iron and steel and employing more than 500 people. In 1956 the co-determination law of 1951 in coal, iron and steel was extended to certain classes of holding company and groups of companies with interests in these industries.

The most recent West German legislation, the Co-determination Act of 1976, extends the provisions of the 1952 Act to companies employing more than 2000 employees although there are differences in detail. The 1976 Act places firms outside coal, iron and steel broadly on a par with those companies which continue to be governed by the 1951 Act. A number of siginficant changes have been introduced, however, and these are worthy of note. Under the new legislation, there is an even number of members and the rigorous procedure for electing the 'odd' man is avoided. However the supervisory board must now elect a chairman and vice-chairman by a two-thirds majority and if this cannot be achieved then the shareholders provide the chairman and the employers the deputy. As the chairman holds a casting vote in the event of deadlock, the balance of power again in the final analysis swings in favour of shareholder interests.

A further interesting innovation lies in the composition of the employee body of representatives. Apart from direct trade union representation, employee representation must now comprise blue-collar, white-collar and senior management representatives. Blue-collar and white-collar workers may elect off their respective separate lists of nominations or off a joint list. The senior management representative(s), while nominated by senior management, are elected by senior management and white-collar workers or, if a joint list arrangement has been agreed for blue-collar and white-collar representatives, by management, white-collar and blue-collar workers.

This attempt to include in the participation machinery the whole spectrum of organisational members has important implications. At the practical level it seeks to overcome a problem which has been noted by the present authors in several British companies; that is the danger that in any system of representative participation, managerial personnel will be squeezed out and left to discover through the normal hierarchical communications, decisions that have been taken without their participation.

What we might call the 'middle management dilemma' was highlighted in a recent report of a survey conducted in Esso Petroleum (UK). Following interviews with 150 managers the report notes that the company was seen as operating different standards of consultation with manual workers compared with managerial groups. The managerial groups felt they were neglected by the company in this regard although, (and possibly because), they wished neither to be unionised nor formally represented.[19]

The 1976 German legislation supplies one answer to the dilemma – although it is reported to be unpopular with both unions and management.[20] The solution is only partial, however, as not all managers can be present at board meetings. Senior and middle management will face continuing difficulties in adjusting to the situation in which their subordinates have access to the board unless the company is able to develop throughout its organisation a distinctively participative style of managing and working and living together.

A further variation which the 1976 legislation introduces over the original Act of 1951 concerns the appointment of the Labour Director to the management board. The new legislation requires that the Labour Director be appointed by the same procedure that is used for the other members of the management board, all of whom are appointed and dismissed by the supervisory board. Appointments and dismissals to the lower board require a two-thirds majority on the supervisory board. As this applies equally to the Labour Director, his appointment is no longer dependent on the majority of employee representatives.

The 1976 Co-determination Act is to be introduced in German industry over a two year period ending in 1978 and there is little that can be said about the operation of that Act. Furthermore, the operation of worker representation on supervisory boards and the methods of appointing labour directors and management boards under the earlier legislation are difficult to evaluate apart from the provisions in the Acts for worker councils (the subject of worker councils are dealt with in the next chapter of this book). Perhaps the most that can be said with any certainty is that the directorial changes have had no major impact. There is little evidence that the fears of management about a dilution of their authority or an implementation of socialist philosophy from board level down have been realised. On the contrary, if any change has been recorded it has been for worker representatives to become more identified with management and with board decisions to the possible detriment of trade unionism. Fürstenberg, for example, notes that worker representatives on the board worked with their fellow directors toward the long-term rationalisation of German coal-mining showing an understanding of 'economic necessities'.[21]

Daniel and McIntosh note, following Blumenthal, that where worker directors have developed an expertise in a particular area, for example pay structures and conditions of employment, there is no evidence that they exploit their position to raise levels of pay in their industry noticeably above that which obtains elsewhere.[22]

German co-determination appears to have had a mildly beneficial effect for each of the parties involved. Worker representatives have not used their position to seek revolutionary change but have had the opportunity to oversee the interests of workers during periods of change. Trade unions have not yielded their negotiating rights but have generally approved of the co-determination principle and sought its extension. Management have not used the worker directors to emasculate other forms of labour representation but have probably gained through a greater appreciation and understanding on the part of representatives, if not workers generally, of their long-term objectives for the company.

The effects of co-determination in Germany appear to have been neither dramatic nor fundamental but to have produced positive gains in areas of consensus. But the operation of co-determination must be seen within the framework set by the two-tier boards. Any evaluation must also be seen in the wider context of German industrial relations. This involves both the structure of industrial relations institutions in Germany and the distinctive traditions and attitudes of the parties involved. The experience of co-determination should also be seen in the wider context of post-war Germany where continuing economic expansion has provided the opportunities for conflicting objectives to be achieved together and where there has been a strong political pressure for equality in worker representation.

If the political analogy is applied to German industrial democracy, however, the co-determination legislation does highlight a number of problem areas. If democracy is to be based on equality of franchise then to use as the vehicle for democracy a board, membership of which is subject to different forms of suffrage, is to build into the movement from the outset inconsistencies which will inevitably strain its subsequent operations. In the West German case equal numbers of seats are given to shareholder and employee interests, (with the important caveats referred to above), irrespective of the numbers to be represented in each case. Subsequent election procedures vary between shareholders and employees to produce further inconsistencies. If parliamentary democracy were to operate in this way, a given number of seats would be allocated in advance of the election to the respective political parties and the parties would elect their nominees to their seats by different voting arrangements.

This is not to criticise the German system of co-determination but rather to draw attention to the dangers and fallacies that exist in an easy assumption that political concepts can be readily transplanted into an industrial context.

The structure and role of boards of directors

The experience with worker directorships in many different contexts is far from conclusive either in terms of its impact as a form of democracy or as a means of enhancing the pursuit of organisational objectives.

Several explanations can be offered for this. Worker directorships are not always introduced with clear or agreed objectives in mind. The Bonser and Scott Bader cases are two examples of unusual clarity of purpose. More typically, the various parties will see particular ways of pursuing their own sectional advantages within the broader scheme. Brannen and his colleagues noted of the British Steel Corporation experiment that it was a compromise, 'an experiment where structure and objectives were unclear even at a formal level'.[23] Batstone has pointed to the varied objectives the different parties have held for schemes of worker involvement in board level decision in a variety of European countries. He notes that 'practice reflects not merely a variety of philosophical and ideological viewpoints but also the pressures imposed by particular types of situation'.[24]

A further difficulty in establishing worker directorships has lain with the nature of the board itself. If workers' representatives are to be involved in strategic decision-making, it is important that they are involved at board level in bodies which really do make such decisions and that they are able to influence such decisions.

Membership of the board of directors is not by itself necessarily the best way of achieving this. Pahl and Winkler have noted that boards of directors may merely be involved in 'ratifications of decisions made earlier and elsewhere .... about which the board had no practical alternative'.[25]

This suggestion is supported by the findings of a British Institute of Management survey published in 1972.[26] In this survey it was reported that in some sixty-five per cent of firms in the sample, boards of directors met monthly and in twenty-three per cent less frequently than that. In only seven per cent did boards meet more frequently. In seventy per cent of the firms, however, a management committee met with a wide ranging brief covering overall company affairs. Such committees typically met fortnightly, weekly or more often than that.

While board meetings tend to be fairly formal affairs with little overt conflict, it is evident that many key decisions are taken in sub-committee and at other, still more informal meetings of key personnel. In the BIM survey it is reported that in one company the five senior executive directors shared one room and it is suggested that 'in many companies, the "management committee" would be in almost continuous informal session regardless of its regular meeting times.'[27]

Additionally, it should be remembered that the board of directors as it exists today is a tightly knit social system. The members of the board are likely to share a common background, a common set of values and broadly common objectives. Surveys of the backgrounds of directors show that they share an educational background which is atypical of the country as a whole. Boards of directors place a high priority on their own task of selecting and 'grooming' future board members while previous board members may continue as non-executive directors after retirement. Other major sources of non-executive directors are family and friends, or else bankers, financiers and accountants. While there will be disagreements between board members, the board as a whole is likely to exist as an integrated social group sharing, at a high level, consensus over basic values.

Given the way boards operate and the inevitable overlap of formal and informal relationships, it is naive to believe that the imposition of worker directors, whether by government or by an enthusiastic managing director, will lead to an immediate change in the way decisions are taken or in the kind and quality of decisions. This has been the finding of Brannen and his colleagues at the British Steel Corporation. The newly appointed directors had to enter a social system in which norms, values and traditional ways of behaving were well established, and worker directors were seen as antipathetic to such values. Brannen *et al* note that forty-seven per cent of directors questioned said they had been positively against the idea of worker directors.[28] Worker directors were clearly identified by other directors with nationalisation and were seen as challenging the value placed on private enterprise.

The worker directors themselves noted the limited role that the board may play in decision-making and the importance of other bodies such as national or divisional committees. In these bodies open debate and effective decision-making seemed to occur, only to be rubber-stamped by the board itself. This problem was perhaps particularly acute in the British Steel situation. Divisional boards had an essentially advisory status *vis-à-vis* divisional managing directors. The worker directors themselves noted this:

'We soon realized that if our contribution was to be confined to attending board meetings monthly or bi-monthly it would be impossible to justify our appointment as worker directors.'[29]

But was it really possible for the worker directors to be attendant at the meetings where horse-trading was done and decisions agreed? Some effort was made to place them on standing and *ad hoc* committees but these tended to be restricted to matters connected only with personnel. Worker directors, if they were accepted at all, were accepted as experts in the personnel function rather than as representatives with a responsibility for a wide range of board activity. They were seen as pursuing an 'effectiveness' role rather than a 'democratic' role and there was conflict between these alternative expectations.

The worker directors were gradually absorbed by the social system that was the board of directors. They were socialised into a realisation of what could and could not be done at board meetings. They received specific training in the directorial role as well as in management more generally. They eventually developed their own roles in interaction with their fellow directors.

Similar processes are reported by Batstone and Davies in their research report for the Bullock Committee. They note that at board meetings in Germany '.... disagreements are rare, voting even rarer and voting split along "capital" and "labour" lines extremely rare'.[30] They note, too, the especially limited powers of the supervisory board in Germany which is formally more restricted than the British unitary board. It is suggested that fuller information and real debate are typically confined to informal situations and sub-committees. Except where worker directors are particularly strong (e.g. where they have 'parity' representation), it is unlikely that they will be present at such meetings.

In considering worker directors, therefore, one must be wary of expecting too much following their appointment. Their impact cannot be separated from the role and structure of the board, and the number of worker representatives involved, as well as the quality and extent of participation at other levels in the organisation.

If one is considering worker directors without supportive participative machinery elsewhere, then it is doubtful if any realistic participation can be achieved at all. If it is achieved it will be because the board is organised to make decisions itself rather than through delegation or because, following delegation, worker representatives are fully involved in sub-committees and able to achieve a degree of acceptability in the informal networks of their fellow directors. This may, however, have implications for the worker directors' relationships with their constituents.

This discussion of the role of the board cannot be separated from the question of board structure. Before closing this chapter a final word must be said about the alternatives of unitary and two-tier boards.

The underlying principle of twin boards as operated in Germany is that a supervisory board appointed by shareholders will in turn appoint a management board which has responsibility not just for day-to-day management but for the determination of policy. The supervisory board, prohibited from involvement in management functions, has the duty of overseeing on behalf of shareholders the managements board's activities. Such supervision is undertaken by inspection of company records and by calling for specific reports from management. Specific measures by the management board may need supervisory board approval and the management board can avoid this by seeking a three-quarters majority of voters directly from the shareholders' meeting.

To many commentators such a two-tier system seems appropriate to the practice of appointing worker directors. By placing worker directors on the supervisory boards, workers share with shareholder representatives, in whatever proportion might be agreed, the task of overseeing the work of the management board. Such a system, moreover, prohibiting as it does direct involvements of managers on the supervisory board (other than as constituency representatives under the 1976 legislation), ensures that each board may carry out its function with clear authority and knowledge of the limits of that authority. The two-tier system seems capable of providing the checks and balances necessary for the sharing of power without damaging the ability of management effectively to carry out their role.

Recent work, however, suggests that the situation may not be as simple as this, and that the distinction between unitary and dual boards may be more apparent than real. Under the two-tier system, the power of the management board may in practice be very great and the power of the supervisory board to check the management board may in practice be quite weak. Davies suggests that German law in fact emphasises the primacy of the management board.[31]

By contrast, the British unitary board operates, as we have already suggested, with a relatively restricted role for the main board and an ongoing managerial activity in the form of sub-committees to the board concerned, not just with day-to-day implementation of policy but with the formulation of long-term, strategic decisions. Davies comments that

> 'the actual distribution of functions between board as such and senior management (under the UK system), is perhaps not very different to that prescribed in German law between supervisory and management boards'.[32]

A major difference between the two systems, however, relates to the ability of the senior management to sit on the unitary board as executive directors in a way that is expressly prohibited in the German two-tier arrangement. The unitary board is thus an integrated whole and, providing worker directors can permeate the social system and are present on the board in sufficient numbers to permit them to join the relevant sub-committees, the unitary board probably offers more power to worker directors than does the dual board system.

The Bullock majority noted the importance of this in their recommendations for a modified unitary board, saying,

> 'it is of the greatest importance that employees should be represented on a board with a real opportunity to influence decision-making. A board would not have such influence if final decisions on major questions were taken outside the board by management ....'[33]

The Report goes on to suggest that in specific areas, the right to the final decision should rest with the board and that this right could not be delegated to senior management.

Other writers, however, have seen advantages in introducing a supervisory board to accommodate representatives of both shareholders and workers. Roberts, for example, has suggested that workers on a unitary board would get involved in specific industrial conflicts as an interest group when such issues were being discussed by the unitary board. He suggests that the functions of controlling and supervising should be separate from the function of managing. A single tier, in his view, would give rise to confusion and conflict.[34]

Against this, the French experience, where companies may choose unitary or dualist structures, has been that after an initial burst of enthusiasm for two-tier boards, there has been a return to the unitary principle. The European Commission explains this in terms of the friction and conflict that has occurred 'in a significant proportion of dualist companies as a result of the supervisory councils having difficulty in confining themselves to control and trespassing on management territory'.[35] Supporters of the unitary principle argue that given flexibility, the single board can avoid demarcation disputes and achieve creative solutions to the individual problems of individual companies.

Conclusion

Whatever form of board structure is finally adopted, certain conditions need to be fulfilled if satisfactory participation in strategic decision-making is to be achieved. Some of these conditions may be adduced from the examples we have quoted and from the subsequent discussion.

Firstly, management should seek to develop relationships on the reconstituted boards that are open and capable of developing trust and confidence between members. Board level representation, furthermore, should help relationships develop beyond the confines of the board. In the Bonser company, although there was no question of a shift in the locus of power, board level relationships were coupled with improvements in management-worker relationships throughout the company. It is important in this respect that the parties develop a consensus about the role and function of the board of which they are members and of their role on the board.

Representation should not be seen as a means of carrying on collective bargaining or individual grievance handling. Nor should it be seen as a means of out-manoeuvring the trade unions. The reconstituted boards must offer some opportunity to influence strategic decisions. If boards frustrate expectations by being further re-structured to avoid the reality of power sharing, relationships can be expected to be embittered rather than improved and a source of continuing conflict rather than of mutual gain and benefit.

Participation at the level of strategic decision must necessarily be indirect – it must take place by means of representation rather than by direct involvement. This produces two further important conditions. There must be adequate feedback by representatives to their constituents and there must also be alternative, complementary forms of participation at other levels within the decision-making hierarchy. The John Lewis Partnership shows how feedback and participation might occur throughout the organisation as well as the difficulties of ensuring that uniformity of practice does not stifle ability through participation materially to influence outcomes. If reporting back becomes a series of bureaucratic procedures, then the involvement in power sharing at lower levels may become no more than a paper exercise. But a vacuum between board level representation and the shop-floor is also unsatisfactory. The problem of maintaining feedback in these circumstances proved a major problem in the British Steel experiment.

One way forward may be through participation at intermediate levels of the decision hierarchy. Such participation is a critical factor in considering arguments for and against unitary or two-tier boards. The danger that worker directors will be isolated on relatively powerless boards is alleviated if there are complementary forms of participation at other decision points in the organisation. Daniel and McIntosh suggest that there is a 'limited though nonetheless important role for employee directors' but they emphasise 'the vital need for an effective system of involvement at lower levels'.[36] The Bullock Committee notes that changes at board level are insufficient. 'What is needed', it suggests, 'is an interrelated structure of participation or joint regulation at all levels of the enterprise.'[37]

It is to the middle level of such an interrelated structure that we now turn.

References

1. E.F. Schumacher, *Small is Beautiful*, Blond and Briggs (London 1973), p. 260.
2. Item 3 of the Preamble to the Constitution of Scott Bader Company Limited.
3. Articles of Association of Scott Bader Company Limited, Number 4 (E).
4. Scott Bader Company Limited, Code of Practice 1972, Paragraph 9.

5. For a discussion of the Kalamazoo Workers' Alliance, see T. Garnier, 'Case Studies in Humanised Management: The Kalamazoo Workers' Alliance', *Industrial and Commercial Training*, (July 1976), pp. 260–64. Also J. Wellens, 'Comments on the KWA Scheme', *Industrial and Commercial Training*, (July 1976),pp. 265–8.

6. G.F. Thomason, 'Workers' Participation in Private Enterprise Organisations' in Campbell Balfour, *Participation in Industry*, Croom Helm (London 1973), pp. 159–160.

7. A. Flanders, R. Pomeranz and J. Woodward, *Experiment in Industrial Democracy*, Faber and Faber (London 1968), p. 187.

8. *Ibid.*, p. 187.

9. *Ibid.*, pp. 82–5.

10. C. Duerr, *Management Kinetics*, McGraw-Hill (Maidenhead 1971).

11. C. Duerr, *Draft Interim Report on the Worker Director: How it Works at Bonser Engineering Limited*, (October, 1975), p. 3.

12. From Extraordinary General Meeting, Bonser Engineering Limited, 23 April, 1976.

13. Articles of Association of Bonser Engineering Limited (1976), Article 124.

14. H. Morrison, *Socialisation and Transport*, Constable (London, 1933), p. 210. Quoted at length in K. Coates and A. Topham, *Industrial Democracy in Great Britain*, MacGibbon and Kee (London 1968), pp. 283–4.

15. *Labour Party Annual Conference Report* (1932), in Coates and Topham, *op. cit.*, p. 289.

16. P. Brannen, E. Batstone, D. Fatchett, P. White, *The Worker Directors*, Hutchinson (London 1976).

17. *Ibid.*, p. 90.

18. *Ibid.*, p. 181.

19. 'Esso Managers Want to Represent Themselves', *Financial Times*, 10 September, 1976.

20. W.A. Tilden, 'Germany', in *Worker Participation: The*

European Experience, Coventry and District Engineering Employers' Association (Coventry 1974), p. 60.

21. F. Fürstenburg, 'Workers' Participation in Management in the Federal Republic of Germany', *International Institute for Labour Studies Bulletin*, 1969.

22. W.W. Daniel and N. McIntosh, *The Right to Manage?*, Macdonald (London 1972), Chapter 8.

23. Brannen *et al*, *op. cit.*, p. 96.

24. E. Batstone, 'Industrial Democracy and Worker Representation at Board Level: A Review of European Experience', in E. Batstone and P.L. Davies, *Industrial Democracy: European Experience*, HMSO (London 1976), p. 11.

25. R.E. Pahl and J.T. Winkler, 'The Economic Elite: Theory and Practice', in P. Stanworth and A. Giddens (Eds.), *Elites and Power in British Society*, Cambridge University Press (London 1974), p. 110.

26. British Institute of Management, *The Board of Directors*, Management Survey Report No. 10, (London 1972).

27. *Ibid.*, p. 4.

28. Brannen *et al*, *op. cit.*, p. 136.

29. *Ibid.*, p. 136.

30. Batstone, *op. cit.*, p. 26.

31. P.L. Davies, 'European Experience with Worker Representation on the Board', in E. Batstone and P.L. Davies, *op. cit.*, p. 54.

32. *Ibid.*, p. 56.-

33. Bullock Committee, *op. cit.*, p. 77.

34. B.C. Roberts, 'Industrial Democracy – The Challenge to Management', Institute of Personnel Management, National Conference, October, 1976.

35. *Employee Participation and Company Structure*, European Communities Commission (Luxembourg, 1975), p. 73.

36. Daniel and McIntosh, *op. cit.*, p. 150.

37. Bullock Committee, *op. cit.*, p. 41.

3 Middle range participation

Introduction

By middle range participation we refer to the fact that in most forms of organisation, once a given minimum size has been exceeded, a range of managerial decision-making activities is to be found at a level above the day-to-day decisions found in primary work groups, but below the broad policy decisions associated with senior management. It will involve certain of the decisions described by Ansoff as 'administrative' together with the managerial, as opposed to the supervisory, element of his 'operating' class of decision. It will involve workers from different levels of the organisation and with different kinds of skills and expertise in organising resources for 'optimum performance'. It is a major theme of this book that effective participation cannot be achieved by concentration on any single level of organisation but must depend on the development of appropriate structures and high trust relationships at every decision-making point within an enterprise.

As we saw in Chapter 2, a great deal of attention has been paid by the press, by government and by academic researchers, to the dramatic changes that are involved in the provision for the appointment of workers or their representatives to company boards. We have also suggested, however, that such board level involvement will achieve little if it is not part of an integrated system of participative institutions and attitudes throughout the enterprise. The achievement of participation at lower points in the enterprise will be less dramatic in impact and requires on the part of its members a great amount of hard work and commitment without any major achievements other than the steady conversion of autocratic and paternalistic styles of behaviour into participative ones, to the mutual benefit of all parties.

Perhaps more than at any other level, participation in the middle range of decision-making is dependent upon the broader systems of industrial relations for its structure, its powers and its ethos. When examining works committees in Great Britain, for example, it is difficult to generalise across all companies in recommending a single package. Companies in manufacturing and service industries, companies with different traditions of industrial relations, with different levels and forms of trade union organisation, with different numbers of plants and numbers of employees will each find different patterns of participation in middle level decisions appropriate and workable and capable of development.

This chapter will begin by examining the twin forms of participation that apply with particular relevance at this level – the exercise of influence through bargaining processes and through various forms of joint consultation and works councils. We will then contrast this combination of institutions in Great Britain with experience of works councils on the Continent of Europe.

Joint consultation and collective bargaining

Joint consultation is but one such approach to decision-making in the middle range. As such it has had a chequered history with periods of considerable boom followed by a lessening of interest and a degree of disillusionment. It is difficult to realise as various schemes are abandoned for failing to offer the participants the decision-making power they sought, that at its origin, the works committee represented a new era. Arising from the exigencies of war and from the new deal promised by Whitleyism, works committees came at the end of a period that had seen the radical syndicalist and guild socialist movements of the left, and the idealistic co-partnerships and industrial schemes of paternalistic entrepeneurs. But Whitley marked the end of one era as well as the start of a new one. As the 1920s progressed, the fire that sparked the experimental idealism of the previous fifty years was quenched by the cold reality of economic depression and the competition and smothering growth of bureaucratic managerialism. As Child expresses it,

> 'most of the discussion given to (works) committees within the management literature by the late 1920s viewed them as *consultative* bodies rather than as any means to afford workers a share in control. In other words there had already been a shift away from Whitleyism, and the democratic ideal which had first accompanied it, towards a concept of 'joint consultation' which was primarily regarded as a useful technique of labour management'.[1]

The inter-war period saw a general decline in plant level joint committees. It took a further war for new life to be breathed into the joint consultation concept. Pressed for, in many ways ironically, by Ernest Bevin, joint production committees were established primarily in engineering and in Royal Ordnance factories.[2] In other industries and, unlike the engineering and ROF examples, they were less likely to make use of union representatives on the employees side.

Nevertheless it was estimated that by the middle of the war, over 4000 joint production committees were operational together with greatly increased trade union activity.[3] The momentum gained during the war carried forward into peace time. A study by the National Institute for Industrial Psychology found that in 1951 over seventy-two per cent of firms taking part in their survey had some form of joint consultation.[4] By 1972 when Clarke and his colleagues did a similar survey, the proportion had dropped to thirty-two per cent.[5]

Explanations for this decline in interest in joint consultation are not difficult to find. Scott, for example, reporting his findings in three Merseyside firms suggested that the process was neither 'joint' nor 'consultative'. It was not joint in that it consisted 'mainly in the submission of problems and requests by employee representatives'.[6] It was not consultative because of the failure of the representatives to develop a relationship with their constituents.

'Representatives were often unaware of any necessity or responsibility to keep in close touch with the rank and file.'[7]

Scott subsequently notes that,

'The employee does not feel that he has a consultative relationship with either his representative or his supervisor. In some ways this means more than that the establishment of joint consultation has failed to influence the day-to-day relationship of most employees .... '[8]

He goes on to suggest that joint consultation, when it fails in this way, can increase dissatisfaction with other shop-floor relationships. Jacques in his study of Glacier Metal similarly found that representatives were seeking to avoid reporting back, with negative effects on the attitudes of rank and file members.[9]

A more fundamental problem facing joint consultation has been the comparison with the way workers and management come together in local bargaining activity. The distinction frequently held by management between consultation and negotiation relates to the amount of conflict involved in the subject matter under discussion. Negotiation implies issues over which there is conflict and which can be resolved only by bargaining and compromise. The point of compromise reflects the relative power of the parties concerned rather than the 'needs of the situation' which are seen in a different light from the different perspectives of the respective parties involved. Consultation cannot satisfactorily deal with matters over which there is such conflict and management has frequently recognised this by establishing separate arrangements for consultation and for negotiation. This operated to the detriment of consultation.

Substantial and major changes have taken place in Britain in the form and content of collective bargaining over the past twenty years and these changes have altered the ways in which we are able to view collective bargaining within a framework of participation.

Up to the mid-1950s in Britain, collective bargaining was mainly conducted at the national level and was predominantly concerned with wages and conditions of employment. In this situation, the idea that collective bargaining could be a vehicle for greater participation within individual companies and plants was difficult to accept. Bargaining was conducted, both from the union and the management side, by parties external to the particular company or plant and the legitimate role of bargaining was extremely narrow.

G. D. H. Cole, writing in 1957, reflects the limited role that collective bargaining then had when he rejects collective bargaining as a substitute for participation saying that,

'Trade Union bargaining, though of the utmost value

in dealing with such matters as standard wage-rates, working hours, and generally applicable conditions of employment, is by no means well adapted for dealing with the host of particular issues that arise in particular workplaces and are of the most immediate concern to the individual worker and the face to face working group'.[10]

But subsequent developments in collective bargaining have shown it to be a most flexible and versatile vehicle by which workers and their representatives may influence managerial decision-making. Several phases may be discerned in this evolutionary process.

The development of productivity bargaining, beginning at Fawley in the late 1950s and early 1960s, simultaneously shifted the locus of collective bargaining from national level to the individual plant and broadened the focus from wages and conditions to a range of working practices.[11] This agreement and others of a similar *genre* did not of themselves establish collective bargaining as a major force for participation but they did lead in the movement by which formal aspects of collective bargaining were seen to be operative within companies and within plants dealing with particular issues appropriate to particular workplaces. At the same time as the productivity bargaining movement was gathering pace, another catalyst for change in industrial relations was at work. Between 1964 and 1967 the Royal Commission on Trade Unions and Employer's Associations (the Donovan Committee) was collecting evidence on the operation of industrial relations in Great Britain and commissioning research. The resulting report together with the series of research papers provide what is probably the most important contribution to date to the systematic study of British industrial relations.

A significant chapter in the report began with the now famous statement that,

'Britain has two systems of industrial relations. The one is the formal system embodied in the official institutions. The other is the informal system created by the actual behaviour of trade unions and employers associations, of managers, shop-stewards and workers.'[12]

Donovan went on to suggest that the two systems were in conflict, that the formal system was becoming increasingly an empty charade and that the informal system could not be forced to fit the formal mould. The informal system moreover, was seen to have many positive advantages in terms of the matters which it could handle. In the light of these and other arguments Donovan came out strongly in favour of a reform of industrial relations which favoured the development of company industrial relations policies.

In the subsequent years, notwithstanding the actions of governments, individual companies have come to recognise the so-called informal system and to move their formal arrangements into line with this. As part of this process we have witnessed the development of productivity bargaining into a more general form of plant level bargaining, the increasing formal power of shop-stewards and the establishment of procedural agreements on a range of topics including redundancy, discipline, grievances and manning. More recently it has been suggested that a succession of fairly tight wage policies by government have diverted shop-stewards away from the traditional hunting grounds of pay to new areas concerned with job regulations and a wider range of company policies.

The result of this expansion and relocation of collective bargaining activity has been to alter the situation that existed in 1957 when G. D. H. Cole was writing, almost beyond recognition. The position in Britain has moved closer to that described by Kuhn in the United States as 'fractional bargaining'.[13] This describes the situation in which the process of grievance handling becomes a dynamic one, characterised by continual local bargaining rather than a formal comparison of the issue with the provisions of an established collective bargain.

Although there is still some distance to go before the mass of firms catch up with the leaders in the field, there are signs that British management is now less inclined to hold tight to the principle of prerogative and is more willing to bargain and negotiate over issues previously considered the inalienable territory of management.

The Ford Motor Company recognizes this, for example, in its evidence to Bullock.

'The realities of industrial life are that in many companies employees, and the trade unions representing them, have already achieved a great deal of participation, through the normal collective bargaining machinery, in those matters which affect their daily working lives .... Employees are able to have a very direct say in, or bring considerable influence to bear on, those decisions which affect not only their conditions of employment but the general actions and plans of, the organisations to which they belong.'[14]

This has been the theme underlying the industrial relations policies of the Delta Metal Company.[15] It is fundamental to the ICI Gloucester case described by Daniel and McIntosh[16] and the philosophy of industrial relations espoused by McCarthy in *Management by Agreement*[17] and, earlier, by Flanders in his evidence to Donovan.[18]

If we contrast this with the discussion of joint consultation above, an important distinction can be made. Participation through the bargaining process has been achieved by the workers' own efforts within trade union organisation. Joint consultation, by contrast, has been given to workers through legislation or through the good graces of management. Plant and company level collective bargaining are therefore independent activities by workers, based on the power of their union organisation. The bargaining can be seen to be for real and is backed by the independent muscle of the union. Joint consultation in the final analysis lacks such independent power. We have already noted the fate of joint consultation in Britain and we may now suggest that its decline has been hastened by the rise of plant level bargaining.

If this is the case, the lessons for future models of indirect, representational participation are clear. Any attempts to run negotiating bodies in parallel with and yet separate from other participative bodies runs the danger of discrediting those participative bodies. Any attempt to institutionalise separately the areas of greater and lesser conflict, of greater and lesser consensus will run the danger of damaging the credibility of the institutions for participation outside the bargaining arena. Management should seek, together with the trade unions, to build on workshop bargaining to establish a single broad encompassing framework for such middle-range participation. This will not be easily achieved and requires more than declarations of good intentions.

It is not possible of course to begin industrial relations anew, with a completely clean slate. Apart from the structural constraints that inevitably feature in any organisation – the dominant technology, the state of the market, the size of the units involved – an organisation carries a legacy of particular industrial relations traditions. This is the starting point for such participation.

Relatively quiet industrial relations or low levels of trade union organisation are not opportunities to *avoid* a single channel scheme, but opportunities for the constructive development of a comprehensive participative programme. As such it will encompass conflict subjects and subjects of traditional consultation.

More turbulent and intensive industrial relations make it more difficult to achieve a combined framework but also more urgent to do so. In such situations it will not be realistic for management to act as though participation could be conducted independent of existing industrial relations and trade union authority. In the printing industry, for example, in motor vehicles, in large parts of the engineering industry, in shipbuilding or in docks, any attempt to establish a separate participation machinery to by-pass the union hierarchy would be fraught with danger which in the long run would rebound on management at the expense of their participation machinery. In situations with traditionally high levels of trade union activity, the development of participation needs to take place by the extension of existing industrial relations activity.

The extension of industrial relations activity in this way gives rise to problems for all parties involved. A strategy for developing participation is reserved for later chapters but some preliminary remarks might be made here. Essentially the difficulty that arises is one of achieving a negotiating and participation stance within the framework of a single meeting. In negotiation the aim is to achieve the maximum for one's members consistent only with an ability to repeat the exercise the following year. The problems that this might create for management are of little concern to the trade union. Management's job is to manage and that includes optimising performances in whatever environ-mental circumstances one is operating. Manage-ment is paid to achieve survival and a degree of prosperity while accommodating trade union demands and negotiated settlements. This process of negotiation involves an inter-personal style which is appreciated by all parties. The need to pitch a claim higher than one realistically expects to achieve; the need to hide from your adversary the true point at which you would be prepared to settle; the need to hold back information which may help your adversary to reach a settlement more favourable to him.

Such styles are quite contrary to those required in a participation setting. The need here is for openness, for a frank exchange of information. Problems face the whole group and action which benefits one party at the expense of the other cannot be considered a satisfactory outcome.

Re-stated in terms which we have already used, negotiation is based on a premise of pluralism, of conflicting objectives and disagreement over means. Participation is based on a premise of consensus, of agreement over objectives and a technical discussion of means. This is essentially the point Walton and McKersie make when they distinguish *distributive* and *integrative* forms of bargaining.[19] The former is a zero-sum situation; a victory for one party involves a defeat for the other. Integrative bargaining occurs in situations which are essentially problem solving and in which all parties gain.

Separating consultation and bargaining into different institutional forms has served to reduce the conflict between these two styles. Using different people in the two situations appears *a priori*, to reduce the conflict still further. In practice, as we have already suggested, the effect of this separation has been for institutions comprising groups with independent sources of power to drive out weaker forms of consultation.

A further disadvantage of joint consultation against plant level bargaining is the extent to which it becomes the victim of its own rules. Joint consultative bodies usually require a certain quorum to meet at specified times. But as Whitehead pointed out forty years ago, problems of management will arise and need to be resolved hour by hour.[20]

Local bargaining is an activity which matches management's needs in this; it too can occur hour by hour as topics of the moment require. Such bargaining offers continuous flexibility compared with the discontinuous, rigidly formal arrangements that have been traditionally part of joint consultation arrangements. As Marsh has noted, work-place bargaining provides 'an imprecise framework for trade union workshop organisation'[21] in which 'it is seldom clear precisely what procedures are to be followed in particular circumstances, except by custom and practice'.[22]

The inconsistencies between the different styles of behaviour appropriate to different tasks and the different balance of power, has led management to adopt a superficially tidy segregation of the activities of consultation and negotiation. The response of trade unions to such a segregation has been to value the form that gives them the greatest freedom of action rather than the formally constrained and contrived circumstances of consultation. The unions have sought to broaden the scope of bargaining activity and the effect has been for the range of topics covered by consultative machinery to be derided as trivial. This in turn brings lower levels of interest and credibility which brings a further contraction. This process of course is particularly true of organisations with high levels of unionisation and growing traditions of plant bargaining.

In discussing the problems of distributive and integrative bargaining, we should be careful not to over-magnify them. As Scott has pointed out, an important element in this area of participation as in others is the attitudes of the parties involved.[23] In a medium-sized foundry and engineering works visited by the authors, shop-stewards happily slipped into 'integrative' styles of behaviour when discussing the technical aspects of a job evaluation scheme, and into a 'distributive' stance when tackling associated questions of pay. The ability of shop-stewards to straddle these styles is attested by such surveys as those of Clegg, Killick and Adams, and McCarthy and Parker which reveal high levels of satisfaction among managers with their dealings with shop-stewards.[24] The Government Social Survey in 1968 showed that the wider the range of issues involving shop-stewards, the more shop-stewards perceived themselves as 'helping' management.[25]

European works councils

It is clear that companies in different situations will have different experiences of participation at this level of decision-making. Such differences are amplified however when one compares companies operating in the cultural, economic, political and legal contexts of Continental Europe and Great Britain. It is facile, however, to assume that Continental Europe operates a single system for employee participation in managerial decision-making. The nation states of Europe have different traditions of industrial relations with important implications for participation. There are different trade union structures for example in the Netherlands, West Germany, Belgium and France. There are different methods of wage determination across Europe and different management styles and responses to trade union activity.

Nevertheless, with this warning in mind one or two general features which distinguish Continental Europe from Britain may be noted before examining some particular provisions in detail.

Perhaps the most important distinction to be borne in mind is the relative importance of law in regulating industrial relations affairs in the rest of Europe compared with Britain. The pattern in many European countries has been for specific legislation on participation, (at Board level as well as in the middle range), to be passed in two stages. The first wave of legislation came in the immediate post-war years and made provisions of varying degrees of compulsion for the establishment of works councils. Following the liberation of Europe much of this legislation appears to have been passed in a spirit of high national consensus and identity. A second wave of legislation has followed in the pressure for participation that has characterised the 1970s and this has usually been more mandatory than the earlier provisions. Again the detail has varied from place to place but Great Britain (and the Irish Republic) have been the odd men out in having no general agreement, either voluntary or legislated, in this area at all up to the time of writing. Not all European countries have followed the two stage pattern: Austria had no works council legislation until 1967, though this was revised in 1973: Italy had works councils on a voluntary basis in the immediate post-war years and has subsequently witnessed the development of a British-style shop-stewards movement at plant level with great influence on works councils: Denmark has achieved plant level participation through voluntary agreement between a highly centralised union movement and employers, but has legislated for Board level participation.

Elsewhere legislation has been more important. Germany has legislated for works councils in 1951, 1952 and 1972 (and, as we have already seen, for further Board level participation in 1976). France has legislation for works committees dating from 1945 and 1968. Belgium's legislation dates from 1948 and 1973. Dutch legislation from 1950 and 1971.

The presence of these legislated and voluntary works councils should also be seen to exist in an industrial relations environment which is quite different from the British situation. The most distinctive feature of British industrial relations as far as the establishment of works councils is concerned is the presence of a strong shop-stewards' movement operating at the level of many plants and factories. Some countries, such as Italy, have more recently adopted this system while in still others, trade unionists see the British approach as offering workers considerable advantages. Tilden notes, in his survey of German works councils, that 'certainly there is more than a touch of envy in German Trade Unionists when they discuss the power and the influence of the shop-steward movement in Britain'.[26]

The German works council system is part of the co-determination legislation already referred to in the discussion of worker directors. These acts require there to be established in all organisations employing five or more persons, a works council representing all employees. The size of the works council is related to the number of employees. It varies from one for organisations with between five and twenty employees, to thirty-one representatives for organisations with between 7001 and 9000 employees. There are two further representatives for every additional 3000 employees. The works council covers all groups of employees irrespective of their union membership and includes both white collar and blue collar workers, but excludes senior management. For works councils of more than nine members a works committee must be formed from within the works council to handle the day-to-day business of the council. Under the 1972 Act there is a requirement for a number of the councillors to be full-time once the plant exceeds 300 employees and all works councillors are entitled, not only to time off to attend council meetings, but to time for appropriate training and educational courses. All costs pertaining to the works councils are carried by the employer.

The works councils have rights to certain information, to consultation and to co-determination. By co-determination is meant the need for management to obtain works council agreement before action may be taken. This applies to such matters as works rules and regulations, starting, stopping times and changes in hours and the operation of welfare schemes. An innovation in the 1972 Act has been rights of co-determination over fixing the rates for incentive payment schemes and the introduction and administration of new payment systems as well as dealing with existing wage and salary administration. The works council has co-determination rights in matters of selection of new personnel and these rights become more precise and detailed in the bigger plants. Works councils have similar rights to co-determine transfers, regradings or dismissals. These are rights to information and consultation on a range of policy decisions concerning expansion into new products, processes and premises together with co-determination of workers rights in problems arising from these decisions.

All this, it should be noted, takes place without any contact between the company and the union *per se*, or shop stewards in the steward's role. The company operates within national union agreements but operates at plant and company level through the participative machinery offered by the works council.

Another example of advanced participation through works councils is to be found in the Netherlands. Once again the operation of this middle range participation can only be understood within the general framework of Dutch industrial relations. These have been characterised in post-war years by high levels of cooperation between unions, employers and the state, and, up to the mid-1960s, by a heavily centralised wage determination system stemming from this tripartite agreement. The early co-operation had surrounded a largely voluntary works council system which had operated since 1950. Following the confusion caused in the late 1960s by the abandonment of centralised wage controls, and the partial breakdown of traditional industrial relations procedures, new legislation, covering works councils and board level participation, was introduced in 1971.

The works councils thus established are to be chaired by the Chief Executive and comprise at least three employee representatives (for firms with twenty-five to fifty employees) and up to fifteen representatives for firms of between 1000 and 2000. Thereafter there are two further representatives for each additional thousand employees up to a total of twenty-five representatives.

As in the German case, the works councils have rights 'to advise' and rights 'to co-determine'. Advisory rights relate to such business policy decisions as the ending of production in particular areas, the closure of plants, the transfer of work to alternative plants, the transfer of ownership of the plant.

Co-determination rights concern matters which might be more narrowly regarded as 'personnel' matters: matters concerned with the contract of employment, pensions, hours of work, holidays, health and safety. Alternatively these matters may be covered by collective bargaining.

These examples may suffice to give the reader an impression of the operations of works councils under formal legislated systems. They are drawn from countries well known for their distinctive approaches to industrial relations. In West Germany a unified trade union structure comprising sixteen unions is unified nationally through the DGB – the German equivalent of the TUC. The conduct of industrial relations is orderly and largely constrained within a legal framework. In the Netherlands, a high degree of national awareness of the country's size and dependence in international trade may have contributed to the low strike record, the tripartite consensus between Unions, employers and the state, and the long period of stable wages policy up to the mid 1960s.

These specific examples, illustrate well the common elements of the European approach to works councils. The general features of this approach may now be contrasted with the British combination of bargaining and consultation described earlier.

British and European experiences compared

As we stated earlier, it is impossible to consider alternative mechanisms for extending participation apart from the broader institutional framework obtaining from country to country and from time to time. This point is well illustrated by the contrasts obtaining between British forms of middle range participation and practice on the Continent of Europe.

A superficial comparison leads to the conclusion that the European countries have made considerable progress by legislating for works councils and equivalent committees while Britain has taken virtually no action. Indeed a pessimistic reading of the situation would suggest that Britain has actually regressed in this area as the numbers of joint consultation bodies have declined or fallen into disuse.

A closer examination of the actual operation of participation in the middle band shows this to be a naive simplification which ignores the difficulties that are encountered in many Continental systems and the value of the distinctive form that such participation has taken in Britain.

Schemes of participation through works councils in most European countries comprise two parts. They involve areas in which there must be consultation between management and works councils and, secondly, areas in which management and works councils co-determine the action that will be taken. As we have seen in the German and Dutch examples, rights to consultation – to receive information, to make suggestions, to offer advice – exist usually in the areas of business policy and economic activity. The rights to co-determination are more normally found in areas of personnel decisions and social matters more broadly. In some of these matters the rights to consultation are quite rigorous. Management may be required to submit written reports on its plans and to justify them in terms of the company's position – its financial position, its investment programme, its production results.

This general European distinction between rights to consultation and rights to co-determination bears some comparison with the British arrangements for consultation and negotiation. Indeed it may be argued that the co-determination rights endowed on many European workers by law are little different from the *de facto* situation obtaining in many British companies as a result of trade union pressure. The rights of Dutch works councils since 1971 to participate in decision-making on work rules, on hours of work or on safety provisions have long been regarded in Britain as legitimate bargaining issues over which unions and shop-stewards should exercise critical influence.

Similarly the German co-determination rights over working hours, holiday arrangements, social amenities, wage scales, productivity bonuses, certain aspects of health and safety at work, job evaluation criteria, policies in recruitment and selection, individual recruitment, promotion, transfer or dismissal etc. could be seen as bringing German workers up to the standards that have been achieved by groups of British workers through trade union action at plant level.

The need for a programme of legislation can, by this argument, be seen simply as a remedial measure to compensate in some countries for the failings of the trade union movement to achieve a voluntary form of co-determination. The British scene, it would then be argued, as a result of its strong unitary trade union movement, with a high level of membership and an improving record of plant level negotiation, has little need for legislation. Indeed the flurry of European legislation in this area since about 1968 brings Europe into line with British practice if not British law.

And this is what one should expect. In the heavily legalistic industrial relations systems that characterise Europe, response to changes in the wider environment must be sought in the law. In the essentially voluntary system that existed in the United Kingdom during the 1950s and 1960s, 'natural' organic developments towards plant level bargaining occurred as an appropriate response to felt needs for more local influence over events in the company. To an extent, this comparison of European and British experience of participation at this level vindicates voluntarism as progressive companies were able to respond with new industrial relations forms ahead of the European legislators.

As with all generalisations, there is an element of truth in this but there are some serious over-estimates of the British achievements. The development of plant level bargaining has been an uneven process and there are today large areas of industry where there have been few if any such developments since the war. Industries with a large proportion of unskilled labour or with white collar, non-unionised labour are in this category. Similarly industries with traditionally high labour turnover or part-time labour would be expected to have paid little attention to the development of single-channel participation at the middle level.

Even within industries which have moved towards a system of plant bargaining, there frequently remain large employers who have not ceded such rights. This can result in major confrontations between the parties over recognition and procedural agreements. Protracted arguments of this kind sour relationships for many years and may ultimately even lead to closure as the parties seek to avoid the loss of face occasioned by a climb-down.

The European legislative approach does have the merit of preventing any group from getting left behind and of avoiding the bitterness and costs to both sides that flow from disputes to establish procedure and basic rights.

A further difficulty with the British approach has been the underlying posture of conflict involved in a union-management confrontation. This has partly resulted, as we have already suggested, in a devaluation of the consultative side of the middle range participation. European legislation has been able to require employers to enter seriously into consultation and in Germany, for example, has required all parties to 'work together .... for the good of the employees and the establishment'.[27] It may be questioned how far one can legislate for the seriousness of a citizen's intentions or compel people to co-operate. It must also be asked how far the European legislation has been able to achieve credibility for the consultative *vis-à-vis* co-determination requirements. Reports of the French experience, for example, suggest a certain disillusionment. Burditt comments on his experience that,

> 'there were no cases (in the companies we visited) where committees could be held up as glowing examples of worker participation in action. Management tended to regard them as a somewhat tiresome necessity. The unions tend to regard them as something of a prop to the capitalist system. Management certainly did not see them as an effective instrument for creating a spirit of co-operation between management and employees and complained that much of the discussion centred around the rather mundane subjects of the state of the toilets and the quality of the food in the canteen'.[28]

In summarising their extensive survey of the European experience of participation the Coventry and District Engineering Employers' Association concludes that,

> 'it is doubtful whether employees in companies with obligatory Works Councils have had any more sense of involvement than their British counterparts and the survey suggests that Works Councils have rarely inhibited managements' freedom to decide and act accordingly'.[29]

These negative findings on the European experience substantiate Daniel and McIntosh's view of the 'ineffectiveness of such bodies all over Western Europe'.[30] Indeed the evidence from Europe at present suggests that a move to a British form of plant bargaining through shop-stewards is almost as likely as the British adoption of formal works council legislation.

Conclusions

If it is accepted that some form of middle range decision-making is an inevitable part of all organisations above a given size and if it is also accepted that participation in such decision-making is desirable in terms of enhanced organisational effectiveness and as preparation for the development of industrial democracy, then the evidence of this chapter would suggest that a number of critical issues need to be recognised and that methods of dealing with them need to be considered in the light of the specific context within which the organisation is operating.

Parties to participation must decide the extent to which consultation and co-determination will feature as the means of dealing with major topics. If co-determination is used, what methods of arbitration can be adopted to avoid the consequences of deadlock? If consultation is used, how can management be shown genuinely to be using the advisory role of the works council?

It is important with such experimental bodies to establish at an early stage the credibility of the institutions. The internal arrangements of the works council might comprise sub-committees which can make considerable progress in co-operative decision making. Sub-committees concerned with safety, health or hygiene, for example, with training, with working conditions, with securing and implementing suggestions or with quality, may quickly achieve results which will encourage participation in more difficult areas.

Such spin-off is only likely to occur if there is a uniform membership basis. Separate bodies for consultation and negotiation with big guns reserved for the latter will devalue the kind of activity undertaken by the former. Institution of middle range participation, in Britain at least, must recognise the reality of trade union power at the plant level and ensure that participative institutions work with trade unions rather than seek to rival them. In companies where trade unions are weak or shop-floor bargaining non-existent, works committees should not be used by management as a means of ensuring their permanent exclusion. The development of such participation bodies must be recognised by management as possible precursors of future trade union participation. Management should seek to train their employee representatives in the practice of co-determination as well as consultation with the same urgency that they would adopt if under direct pressure from trade unions. There is, indeed, a sense in which the strongly unionised firm, with a tradition of tough yet constructive industrial relations, may find the introduction of works committees to handle the whole range of participation at this level, easier than firms without any traditions of shop-steward organisation.

The fundamental change that must be established if participation at this level is to succeed is a change in attitudes. This refers to the attitudes of all parties to the participative process, to management and to trade union representatives. Scott notes that harmonious relationships will not be achieved by committee. Nor will they be achieved simply by agreement between representatives. They require 'prior changes in the attitudes and behaviour of at least a majority of all the persons involved'.[31]

One of the disadvantages of a series of tight legal prescriptions governing the constitution, powers and responsibilities of work councils is the inflexibility this gives rise to over time. One might expect uncertainty and suspicion in the early days matched by a tendency to lean on legal definitions. In a successful scheme, however, a management awareness of the need for effective action would develop an ability to use the opportunities offered by middle range participation successfully to pursue its tasks. Similarly trade union representatives should seek to pursue the interests of their members within the context of organisational success and as early achievements are recorded and insecurities oversome, the development of attitudes may be expected to occur which far outstrips legal definitions. Little purpose will be served by parties debating the dividing line between consultation and co-determination if they are in consensus on fundamental objectives; little purpose will be served if such consensus is lacking.

The situation on this front is far from gloomy. Despite sensational press reports, statistics in Britain reveal a relatively low level of strikes over the greater part of industry and commerce. Relationships between the vast majority of shop-stewards and managers are peaceful and constructive. Participation involves only an extension of these relationships in a spirit of trust and mutual respect which does not seek to threaten the other party but to advance areas of common concern to both parties.

The development of favourable attitudes to assist the development of participation in the middle range, will not be confined to developments at this level alone. We have said that the success of works committees will be related to the attitudes held by participants. These attitudes, however, are formed not only by events at the middle level but by decisions, which may be achieved through participation, at more senior levels – including board level. These attitudes are also influenced by the quality of working life at the most basic level of all, the level of the individual job. It is to the extension of participation at this level that we now turn in the next chapter.

References

1. J. Child, *British Management Thought*, Allen and Unwin (London 1969), p. 76.
2. See I. McGivering, D. Matthews, W.H. Scott, *Management in Britain*, Liverpool University Press (Liverpool 1960), p. 100.
3. International Labour Organisation, *Co-operation in Industry*, (Geneva 1951), pp. 33–34. In McGivering *et al*, *op. cit.*, p. 100.
4. National Institute for Industrial Psychology, *Joint Consultation in British Industry*, Staples Press (London 1951), p. 21.
5. R.O. Clarke, D.J. Fatchett, B.C. Roberts, *Workers' Participation in Management in Britain*, Heinemann (London 1972), p. 73.
6. W.H. Scott, *Industrial Leadership and Joint Consultation*, University of Liverpool Press (Liverpool 1952), p. 148.
7. *Ibid.*, p. 150.
8. *Ibid.*
9. E. Jacques, *The Changing Culture of a Factory*, Tavistock (London 1951), p. 317. For a further critical review of the operation of joint consultation, this time in the coal industry see P. Anthony, 'The Coal Industry', in Campbell Balfour, *Participation in Industry*, Croom Helm (London 1973).
10. G.D.H. Cole, *The Case for Industrial Partnership*, MacMillan (London 1957), p. 14.
11. See A Flanders, *The Fawley Productivity Agreements*, Faber and Faber (London 1964).
12. Royal Commission on Trade Unions and Employers' Associations *Report*, HMSO (London 1968), p. 12.
13. J.W. Kuhn, *Bargaining in Grievance Settlement*, Columbia University Press (New York 1961).
14. Memorandum from Ford Motor Company Limited to The Committee of Inquiry on Industrial Democracy, (March 1976), p. 2.

15. Richard O'Brien, 'Plant Procedure and Agreements: A Case Study', in S. Kessler and B. Weekes (Eds.), *Conflict at Work*, BBC Publications (London 1971), pp. 75–82.
16. W.W. Daniel and N. McIntosh, *The Right to Manage?*, Macdonald (London 1972). Also S. Cotgtove, J. Dunham, C. Vanplew, *The Nylon Spinners*, Allen and Unwin (London 1971).
17. W.E.S. McCarthy and N.D. Ellis, *Management by Agreement: An Alternative to the Industrial Relations Act*, Hutchinson (London 1973).
18. For a statement of these views see the twin books by Allan Flanders, *Industrial Relations: What is Wrong with the System*, Faber and Faber (London, 1965), and *Collective Bargaining: Prescription for Change*, Faber and Faber (London 1967).
19. R.E. Walton and R.B. McKersie, *A Behavioural Theory of Labor Negotiations*, McGraw-Hill (New York 1965).
20. T.N. Whitehead, *Leadership in a Free Society*, Oxford University Press (Oxford 1936).
21. A.I. Marsh, Royal Commission on Trade Unions and Employers' Associations, Research Paper No. 2, *Dispute Procedures in British Industry*, HMSO (London 1966), p. 18.
22. *Ibid.*, p. 19.
23. Scott, *op. cit.*, p. 149.
24. H.A. Clegg, A.J. Killick, R. Adams, *Trade Union Officers*, Blackwell (Oxford, 1961); Royal Commission on Trade Unions and Employers' Associations, Research Paper No. 10, *Shop Stewards and Workshop Relations*, HMSO (London 1968).
25. Government Social Survey, *Workplace Industrial Relations*, HMSO (London 1968).
26. W.A. Tilden, 'Germany' in Coventry and District Engineering Employers' Association, *Worker Participation: The European Experience*, (Coventry 1974), p. 69.

27. R. Harrison, *Workers' Participation in Western Europe 1976*, Institute of Personnel Management (London 1976).
28. A.R. Burditt, 'France', in Coventry and District Engineering Employers' Association, *op. cit.*, p. 56.
29. Coventry and District Engineering Employers' Association, *op. cit.*, p. 119.
30. Daniel and McIntosh, *op. cit.*, p. 100.
31. Scott, *op. cit.*, p. 149.

4 Direct participation

Introduction

The forms of participation discussed in the last two chapters, board level and middle range participation, while important in a total company approach, both fail to involve the rank and file employee on any continuing basis.

Although it is true that attempts to involve workers in a greater range of decisions about their work can have only limited success for as long as higher levels of decision continue to be taken unilaterally, the reverse is also true. Efforts to extend participation at the higher levels alone run the risk that, by providing the ordinary worker on the shop-floor and in the office with opportunities to participate only at the occasional election, he will become apathetic about the whole exercise. One of the failings of political democracy has been its inability to provide for the citizen any continuing role in the institutions of government. Through direct participation, this mistake can be avoided in the work situation and a surer foundation laid for future democratic developments.

This point was made in one company known to the authors, where the managing director commented on Scott Bader, saying,

'One of our visitors surprised us by saying that in some ways we have achieved more than Scott Bader. As the person knew quite a lot about Scott Bader, and we

would have considered our efforts very modest
compared with theirs, we asked him to enlarge on this
statement. His reply was that in our company, a lot of
people have a say about the way in which their own
job is organised, whereas this is not the case at Scott
Bader. To a lot of people this is more meaningful and
important than the ideas of the Scott Bader
Commonwealth.'

We would emphasise again that the view of this book is
that both direct and indirect forms of participation need to
be involved in the development of truly satisfactory models
of participation.

In this chapter we will introduce some of the academic
research which has given impetus to subsequent
experimentation in work situations. We will then examine
some experiments in which workers have been given
opportunities for a considerable extension of direct
participation in carrying out their everyday work task.

Direct participation and group dynamics

An important element in programmes of job re-design has
been a recognition that work is a social activity. Workers are
members of groups, work is sometimes completed by
groups and group membership carries implications for
individual attitudes and behaviour.

Much academic research with implications for direct
participation was concerned to explore the nature of this
interplay between group membership and individual
action. Studies of different groups noted what happened
when managers attempted to over-ride group values. They
demonstrated the enormous benefits accruing to persons
who could harness and work with social norms and the
reinforcement that the group offered. Such matters were at
the heart of Elton Mayo's findings at the Hawthorne plant.

But they were also being developed by other researchers quite outside the industrial setting with results that were to have considerable significance for management and supervision.

Two such studies conducted by Kurt Lewin will illustrate the relevance of studies of group dynamics to the question of supervisory style. In the first of these, Lewin and his colleagues examined behaviour in a boys' club when the boys were subjected to different leadership styles.[1] Different researchers at different times undertook democratic, autocratic and *laissez-faire* styles – thus neutralising as far as possible the effect of the researchers' personalities. In the autocratic group, boys were told what activities would be taken and in the *laissez-faire* situation they were left to their own devices to find things to occupy themselves. In the democratic groups the leader called for suggestions from the group, acted to help the group achieve its objectives, pointed to alternative actions and suggested likely outcomes. Perhaps the most notable feature of this experiment lay in the activities of the groups when the leaders were absent. While the *laissez-faire* and autocratic groups ceased activity and used the absence of the leader to indulge in 'horseplay', the democratic group showed a greater willingness to stick at their mutually agreed activities. There was not a complete correlation, however, between leadership style and group behaviour and we shall return to some consequences and implications of these disparities below.

Another study by Lewin which shows the power of the group to achieve change concerned groups of housewives.[2] The opportunity for this study occurred in the USA during World War II when it was public policy to encourage consumption of such 'soft' meats as kidney, liver, or heart and to reduce consumption of traditional American favourites such as beefsteaks. Groups of volunteers, (organised for home-nursing during the War), were subjected to two different treatments. One set of groups were given 'attractive lectures' describing the need to change consumption patterns as part of the war effort and the nutritional value of the alternative foods. This was supplemented by 'hand-outs' which described recipes and the lecturer talked of the success she had had with such dishes in her own family.

A further set of groups were subjected to an alternative treatment in which the respective groups entered into discussion among themselves over the value of the different meats and the need to change consumption patterns. They were then given similar recipes and advice by the lecturer. A follow-up study showed that while only three per cent of the first set of groups, who received only the lecture, reported subsequently serving a new kind of meat, some thirty-two per cent of the discussion groups changed their habits in this way. In all cases, the volunteers had been subjected to only forty-five minutes experimentation.

These two studies by Lewin show alternative ways in which groups may be 'managed' and the potential that exists where a participative approach to primary groups is used. Such evidence, moreover, is not confined to social groups outside the work situation. Their general findings have been confirmed by direct experiment and by widespread observation of group relationships in industry. A key study in this area was conducted shortly after the war by Coch and French.[3]

This research, conducted in the American Harwood Corporation, a pyjama manufacturer, showed that the ideas of Lewin had a relevance for the conduct of management-labour relations. The study was concerned with resistance to change. The nature of the product and the competition made necessary frequent changes in style which involved new operations. Such changes were disliked by the workers and it was frequently the case that they failed to reach a minimum efficiency level before further changes were introduced. As workers were operating on piece rate, management had guaranteed a minimum take home pay. Nevertheless by speeding up the rate at which they assimilated new skills, workers could have increased their earnings.

The experimenters believed that motivation rather than skills was the major factor. Re-organisation of work frequently involved transfer of workers and a new rate-setting operation by work-study. Workers believed that high piece-rate earnings induced management to bring in changes which permitted them to adjust the rate. Strong group norms operated among workers to keep production below a level acceptable to the group.

The researchers divided the workers into four groups – three experimental groups and a control. A change involving a move to new jobs was introduced and members of the control group were treated in the normal way. The modified job and the new piece rate were presented to a meeting of the workers. They were told that the change was necessary to meet competitors' conditions. The time study man explained the new rate in detail and answered questions which arose. The meeting was then ended and the women returned to work.

In the experimental groups, a meeting was held with all the operators involved before any change was made. Coch and French then describe the procedure as follows:

'The need for change was presented as dramatically as possible, showing two identical garments produced in the factory; one was produced in 1946 and sold for 100 per cent more than its fellow in 1947. The group was asked to identify the cheaper one and could not do it. This demonstration effectively shared with the group the entire problem of the necessity of cost reduction. A general agreement was reached that savings could be effected by removing the 'frills' and 'fancy' work .... '[4]

Management then presented its plan for the new job and the associated piece-rate and this was approved by the group 'though no formal group decision was reached'.

In experimental group A the above procedure was followed by a further meeting with selected operators who were to be specially trained. 'They displayed a co-operative and interested attitude and immediately presented many good suggestions.' In the other two experimental groups, all the members went on to the special training.

The control group showed the usual drop in production and never returned to their former levels for the thirty-two days that the experiment lasted after the change. They showed aggression and hostility against management, grievances were filed against the new piece rate and a number of workers left the company.

In the experimental groups B and C production levels recovered almost immediately after the change and went on for the remainder of the experimental period to exceed the output levels obtaining prior to the change. In experimental group A, recovery to former levels of production took longer, but that group also exceeded eventually its former production levels. Coch and French report some initial difficulties in supplying work to this group and it is difficult to know whether this or the slightly different experimental conditions produced the differences in results.

Experimental results of this kind in the immediate post-war years appeared to confirm many of the Hawthorne findings. The group was a source of sentiments which could operate for or against the enterprise. Attempts by management to impose its will in an authoritarian way not only excluded the contribution that working groups could make to management decision-making, but were likely to result in antagonistic sentiments being expressed towards management. Democratic or participative approaches to primary groups, whether they are working groups or not, seem likely, on the basis of the limited evidence, to be associated with increased levels of commitment to decisions.

An additional stream of thought which has strongly influenced the development of forms of direct participation has been about the nature of human motivation. The central figure who has dominated this topic for the past thirty years is Abraham Maslow.[5] He postulated a hierarchy of needs and suggested that, with some exceptions, individuals only became motivated by needs at the upper end of the hierarchy when 'lower order' needs have been satisfied. The five groups of needs may be pictured diagrammatically as in Figure 4.1.

Figure 4.1   Maslow's Hierarchy of Needs

Self-actualisation needs	V
Esteem needs	IV
Belongingness and love needs	III
Safety needs	II
Physiological needs	I

The most basic needs, the physiological, must be satisfied, at least in part, before an individual will turn his attention to higher order needs. Safety needs may be considered to be partly physical and partly psychological. Esteem needs similarly divide into two parts – esteem from other people and self-esteem. At the top of the hierarchy, the need for self-actualisation is described by Maslow when he says,

> 'a musician must make music, an artist must paint, a
> poet must write if he is to be ultimately at peace with
> himself. What a man *can* be, he *must* be.'[6]

Maslow continues by defining self-actualisation as,

> 'man's desire for self-fulfillment, namely .... the
> tendency for him to become actualised in what he is
> potentially'.[7]

There has been a generally uncritical acceptance of
Maslow's ideas and we shall return to this later in the
chapter. The assumption that 'self-actualisation' is a 'good
thing' for all has been a driving force behind calls for job
enrichment and other similar forms of direct participation.
There is some confusion, however, between the view that
self-actualisation is a moral right to which every worker is
entitled, and that it is a means of raising job satisfaction
from which greater productivity might be expected.

An emphasis on the ways in which primary groups can
influence attitudes and behaviour, and on the intrinsic or
instrumental value of self-actualisation have been major
themes in the development of schemes for direct
participation. Superficially at least, these two themes seem
to be mutually supportive. Allowing primary groups of
workers to participate in a wider range of decisions should
also provide some opportunity for greater self-actualisation
by avoiding the artificial and frequently frustrating barriers
erected by the principles of Scientific Management and high
levels of task specialisation. Increasing levels of direct
participation should also assist the fulfilment of Maslow's
middle order needs. Extending the role of the primary
group in production and in other ways and also changing,
therefore, the style of supervision, should contribute to
satisfaction of needs for belonging and for esteem. In the
light of all the above, changing production methods to
allow greater direct participation should generally increase
levels of worker satisfaction. But does it, and what are the

implications for productivity and other measures of organisational effectiveness?

Organisations all over the world have sought to implement lessons from the range of ideas discussed here. They have used all kinds of measures which we can discuss under the general heading of job re-design.

Job´re-design

The re-design of jobs has taken many forms which may be seen as more or less radical. At one extreme it has simply amounted to job rotation or, more adventurously, to job enlargement. Alternatively it could involve a fundamental redesign of the work process involving new capital equipment, new factory lay-outs or even new factories. It has been applied in offices where workers are allowed more freedom and a greater range of decision. It has been applied to supervisor-worker relationships, where close supervision, centred primarily on getting work completed, has been replaced by supervision centred on allowing the employee to accomplish agreed objectives in the most appropriate way.

We have suggested that job rotation is a relatively timid approach to the opportunities offered by job re-design. This perhaps depends on the way in which it is implemented and management's objectives. Transferring workers from one meaningless task to another may break the boredom for a time but it is doubtful if it will release new motivations or improve the workers' commitment to the task.

Butteriss, however, reports that Aspro Nicholas use job rotation to some advantage.[8] Moreover, the use of job rotation to develop in a group of workers a range of skills which permits the subsequent extension of the range of work done by the group and the organisation of that work must be classed quite separately from the narrow meaning more usually ascribed to the term.[9]

Job enlargement might similarly be seen as a relatively

limited concept. Joining two boring and meaningless tasks together could conceivably make things worse rather than better. One way of measuring job enlargement is in terms of 'cycle time'. By joining jobs together, the length of time before the worker repeats the task can be extended. But for some people, increases in the cycle time are sufficient to prevent automatic responses to the task, which leave the worker free to talk or to daydream, but do not really remove the fundamental boredom. In these circumstances, job enlargement can be a source of lower efficiency. One study has suggested that increases in cycle time from one to three minutes, to ten to fifteen minutes are likely to reduce rather than raise efficiency on light assembly work.[10] Similarly, a cycle of sixty to ninety minutes in this type of work is seen to be too great. The ideal for such situations is suggested as twenty to twenty-five minutes. In heavier assembly work, the report finds that longer periods of forty-five to sixty minutes can be used with advantage.[11]

But these techniques do not really implement the theoretical lessons about the significance of groups discussed above, nor do they do much to move workers up Maslow's motivational hierarchy.

Schemes which do these things might more properly be described as job enrichment. Job enrichment is a form of job re-design which does not simply lengthen the cycle time but also adds to the job content a greater degree of autonomy. Often building on the small, primary group, workers may become responsible for carrying out their own maintenance tasks, for setting up their machines or for carrying out quality control. Groups may become responsible for setting their own targets, and for allocating work tasks, within overall departmental schedules. They may also contribute to establishing such schedules. Such forms of job enrichment represent patterns of direct participation. Ultimately they involve a shift in authority and responsibility for decision-making which has implications for managerial and supervisory practice.

Companies in many countries are now experimenting with different forms of job enrichment but the extent to which management is able or willing to make such changes varies from place to place.

Experiments in increased autonomy

Morse and Reimer have reported an attempt by an insurance company in the United States to extend the decision-making powers of a group of clerical workers.[12] A large department in a non-unionised insurance company applied different management styles to different groups. The department comprised four divisions engaged in parallel routine clerical activities. Divisions A and B were subjected to programme I, which the researchers referred to as the autonomy programme. Increasingly participative methods of desision-making were introduced. Delegation took place wherever possible between the most senior executives and the routine clerks and encompassing the several levels between. Furthermore, supervisors and clerks were allowed to make co-decisions on a range of personnel topics such as holidays, lunch arrangements or overtime.

In the other two divisions, divisions C and D, programme II was implemented which the researchers referred to as the hierarchically controlled programme. In these divisions the role activity of senior management in making decisions increased. More power accrued to these levels and the routine clerical workers were placed increasingly in the position of simply receiving information about decisions as it was passed down the line.

The researchers examined two main hypotheses. One concerned the relationship between the two programmes and levels of satisfaction, and the second was concerned with the relationship between the programmes and productivity.

After a control period of six months, initial benchmark measurements were taken. The experimental conditions then operated for a further twelve months after which further measurements were made to test the research hypotheses. The hypotheses concerning levels of satisfaction and the experience of the respective programmes were largely confirmed. Under programme I, the autonomy programme, relationships became generally more co-operative and friendly. Perceived levels of self-actualisation increased under programme I and decreased under programme II. (Under programme I the job was seen as more of a 'real challenge', as giving the individual more opportunity to try out his or her own ideas, as giving people a chance to do what they are best at). Individuals in programme I reported increased levels of satisfaction with their relationships with different levels of management and increased satisfaction with the company and with their job. Individuals on programme II showed decreased levels of satisfaction in these areas.

The researchers conclude that,

> 'taking all of these results on the attitudinal questions together, the first hypothesis (on levels of satisfaction) would appear to be verified. Increasing local decision-making increased satisfaction, while decreasing the role of rank and file members of the organisation in decision-making decreased it.'[13]

The second hypothesis that related increased decision-making under programme I to higher levels of productivity – and that related programme II to lower levels of productivity – was not upheld. Programme I showed an increase in productivity of about twenty per cent while the divisions involved in programme II increased by twenty-nine per cent. The researchers, however, do not attach a great deal of significance to this. Output is determined, not by individual departments, but by the flow of work in the organisation as a whole. Changes in productivity were largely the result of the number of people employed.

'The hierarchically controlled programme reduced staff costs by ordering reductions in the number of employees assigned to the tasks. Increases in productivity in divisions C and D were brought about as simply as that'.[14]

Changes were brought about differently in divisions A and B as follows:

'The autonomy programme increased the motivation of the employees to produce and thus they did not feel the need for replacing the staff-members who left the section. In addition they were willing to make an effort to try to outplace some of their members in other jobs which they might like.'[15]

Thus the reduction in staff that produced the different changes in productivity came about in different ways – on the one hand through hierarchical command and on the other through group decision. In the event the hierarchical command produced better levels of productivity but Morse and Reimer question how long this superiority could last. This view was later echoed by Rensis Likert when he suggests in his book *The Human Organisation* that autocratic forms of management may achieve immediate results but only at the expense of long-term effectiveness.[16] The kind of improvements in levels of satisfaction recorded by Morse and Reimer are of long-term significance to the company. Apart from the improvement they represent in the quality of life experienced by employees, they may also be seen as adding to the 'human assets' of the company which will stand the company in good stead during future crises and at times of organisational change. Some evidence of this was already apparent in the Morse and Reimer study. Although labour turnover for other than personal reasons was low in the insurance company, nine persons resigned because of dissatisfaction or to take other jobs. All nine were from the hierarchically controlled divisions C and D.

Nevertheless, the view that the divisions participating in the autonomy programme would eventually better the other two divisions in terms of productivity is no more than an expression of opinion by the researchers. Managers might argue that in the here and now, the participative programme failed to match the results obtained by traditional methods of management.

Similar experiments to extend the autonomy of individual workers and groups of workers have been conducted elsewhere in the United States. In Great Britain, the most celebrated example of job enrichment has been that at ICI. The changes introduced there are described in detail by Paul and Robertson.[17] They involved attempts to extend the autonomy of a wide range of occupational groups. Sales representatives were given greater freedom in planning their work, in deciding how to report their findings, in settling customer complaints and even, within limits, in determining prices.

Similar extensions to autonomy were developed for the special problems attaching to other occupational groups. Experimental officers in research and development were given more discretion in planning and executing projects. Draughtsmen were organised in groups which similarly had more organised responsibilities for carrying through complete projects. Foremen were not allowed to become impoverished by these experiments. They too were given more autonomy from middle management, with more freedom to take decisions on a range of issues that affected their work both in technical areas and in matters of man-management.

Paul and Robertson report considerable success for these experiments both in terms of job satisfaction and improved effectiveness in the various areas affected. They suggest that such experiences might be successfully repeated elsewhere.

Both the Paul and Robertson, and the Morse and Reimer studies have involved predominantly white collar groups.

They have also been efforts to adapt existing situations into more participative forms. Two studies will now be described which attempted to use the opportunities provided by the building of new plants to extend the direct participation of manual workers in a range of decisions surrounding their work.

Job enrichment in total organisations

Richard Walton has described the experiences of a company manufacturing pet food, which decided to implement certain behavioural science findings on job enrichment in the building of a new factory.[18] Planning and design took over two years and the factory that resulted had a number of key features.

1. Autonomous work groups Rather than assigning individuals to highly specified roles, thought out in advance and co-ordinated via the management system with the remainder of the organisation, 'self-managed work teams' were given responsibility for large segments of the production process. A team comprised seven to fourteen members including a team leader. Walton described the range of tasks that a team might be involved in:

> 'the processing team's jurisdiction includes unloading, storage of materials, drawing ingredients from storage, mixing and then performing the series of steps that transform ingredients into a pet food product'.[19]

The teams were thus involved, not simply in an extension of a specialised task, but in the responsibility and decision-making involved in the organisation and carry-through of a major part of the total product-process. This would involve the team in such diverse activities as selection of new employees to replace departed team members, tackling team members who are failing in their obligations, coping with manufacturing problems within and between teams.

2. Integrated support functions It follows from the above that the teams contained their own 'staff' functions. For the most part they carried out their own maintenance, quality control and personnel activities.

3. Challenging job assignments The range of work thus covered by the team meant that it was possible to avoid one person having entirely undemanding jobs. The allocation of tasks within the team was the responsibility of the team and they were constantly distributing and re-distributing tasks.

4. Job mobility and rewards for learning Pay increases over the single job classification for all employees were limited to the number of jobs in the team and in the plant that the individual had learnt.

5. Facilitative leadership Team leaders were responsible, not for planning, directing and controlling in the style of traditional foremen, but for encouraging team development and ensuring group decision-making.

6. 'Managerial' decision information for operators In order that the teams may make group decisions, management information was now widely disseminated.

7. Self-government for the plant community Plant rules were allowed to evolve from 'collective experience'.

8. Congruent physical and social context There was no emphasis in the plant on division 'status symbols'. There were common car-parking arrangements, canteen arrangements and toilets for office and manual employees. There was a common entrance for all employees and common decor throughout.

9. *Learning and evolution* The system was constantly reviewed and adjusted in terms of 'the plant's productivity and its relevance to employee concerns'.

Walton believes that the extra start-up costs attributable to these innovations was very small and certainly recovered in the first year of operation. After eighteen months of operation the plant was reported to have 'saved' $600,000 through reductions in variable manufacturing costs while its fixed overheads were thirty-three per cent lower than in the plant it replaced. While not all this can be said to be due to the new organisational form, quality rejects were reduced by ninety-two per cent, absenteeism by nine per cent and reported levels of job satisfaction and commitment were high.

Perhaps the best known example of participation through job enrichment is that of the new Volvo car factory at Kalmar in Sweden. Volvo have a record of experiment in improving working conditions, by both technological innovation and by social change in the form of small development groups, extending over many years.[20] In their factory at Olofstrom, for example, Volvo began in 1970 to establish new methods of supervision in which 'supervisors act less as authority figures and more as sources of assistance and guidance'.[21] New technology has been designed to eliminate where possible the most boring work and elsewhere the development of buffer inventories has given workers new freedom and discretion.

Such experiences in their many factories gave Volvo a fund of knowledge on which to draw in designing their new plant at Kalmar. Job enrichment through new job design may be seen to have begun with the building itself. The intention has been to establish many small workshops within the large plant. Accordingly, the irregularly shaped factory has many corners and many outside walls with windows giving views of the outside world. The building permits many small groups to operate and work is brought to them on a battery-powered wagon. The wagon bearing the motor car on which the group is working is thus stationary in the group's work-bay rather than continually moving on the assembly line. The group can decide for itself how to divide the work and deploy its members.

The Kalmar plant is estimated to have cost some ten per cent more than an equivalent-sized conventional factory. Furthermore it carries extra overheads in the additional stocks of parts necessary for the system. It is perhaps still too early to judge the results of this venture but reports suggest that the plant is certainly no less efficient than conventional assembly plants and, after nine months in operation, workers were reportedly of the view that the new plant was overwhelmingly superior to the old.

New forms of participation in old plants

As a final example of direct participation we will examine the ways in which another Swedish company, by a process of gradual change involving mistakes and reversals, eventually produced new forms of work organisation within its established plant and with its original technology.

Jan Edgren has described these developments at the Granges Weda die-casting foundry at Upplands Vasby.[23] The plant, which is part of Granges AB, a large multinational, manufactures die-cast zinc and aluminium products. The die-casting is done by injecting molten metal under pressure into a steel mould which, when the metal is cold, is opened and the casting removed. Although a repetitive job, it is one requiring skill and experience. The men involved may be casters or set-up men. The latter group are the more highly skilled and are usually promoted from among the casters. They set up machines, fit tools and carry out minor repairs.

The casters and set-up men had been on a piece-work payment system. In July 1969 this was converted to a time basis and, although some workers gained, a number suffered a considerable loss of earnings. Management, who had hopes for improvements in productivity, labour turnover, accident rates and scrap waste, found little improvement in any of these. Productivity and labour turnover in particular deteriorated considerably.

Management subsequently decided to act to get another form of payment system and to couple this with other changes it had been contemplating in the organisation of production.

After due negotiation with shop stewards, the plant moved in February 1971 to a group form of production and to monthly premium wages. A fixed wage represented seventy per cent of pay and the remaining thirty per cent related to monthly output and was divided among all employees according to the time they had worked.

The group form of production meant that instead of casters working individually, fixed production groups were created around sets of machines, each having its own set-up men. Within the groups, 'first-men' were appointed from among the more skilled men, and became responsible for all activity within the group. The foreman's responsibilities at the day-to-day level were thus decentralised to the group and he was left with longer term responsibility for the total shop. Within the production groups, the first-man worked alongside the other men and all tasks were to become interchangeable.

Additionally, the first-men were members of a joint production committee responsible for production planning. This committee also comprised the production manager and his assistant, the planner, the foreman and the shop-steward. It was a means by which the production group was involved in higher levels of decision-making.

Implementation of this dual system – monthly premium wages and production groups – was followed by considerable improvements in productivity and reductions in labour turnover, scrap loss and absence rate.

After operating the scheme for some time, dissatisfactions began to appear. Some of these concerned the role of the first-man. Complaints were made that they were reverting to the role of foreman and becoming middle men between the workers and the decision-making. They were not reporting back to their production groups.

As a result, some first-men were replaced by casters on the joint production committee and this representation was rotated. Also the selection of first-men was democratised and a form of election instituted.

This study has been discussed at some length because it holds some important lessons within the larger theme of this book. The company introduced changes to deal with problems it was facing. These changes evolved over time and emerged from participative discussions between men and managers. Moreover, greater participation at the level of the task inevitably related to participation at higher levels. Even in establishing participation within an established plant and technology, effective participation at one level held implications for the conduct of the wider organisation.

Reservations and conditions

We shall examine more fully in the next chapter, the kind of reservations that should be kept in mind in thinking about participation. For the present, however, we will note the caution with which many academic observers have regarded various forms of direct participation. Strauss, for example, while generally sympathetic to participation, has expressed many of the doubts that social scientists have.[24]

Other researchers have produced openly contradictory results. We have already noted the ambivalent findings of Morse and Reimer. Katz and his colleagues at Michigan had earlier found that while 'employee centred' leadership was associated with higher levels of output, job satisfaction *per se* was not associated with productivity and indeed if any trend could be noted it was for lower levels of job satisfaction to be related to higher productivity.[25]

Other researchers have produced similarly ambiguous findings. Pelz, in a study of a public utility in the United States found that significant groupings did not respond to supervisors who practised 'employee centred' leadership.[26]. He found, for example, that older workers with lower levels of education failed to produce high morale in the face of such supervisory practices. A review of twenty studies made between 1945 and 1965 showed correlations between job satisfaction and performance criteria of between – .31 and .86 with a median correlation of .14.[27]

In order to put the research on direct participation in context, we shall examine some alternative approaches to motivation and consider the wider context in which such participation has occurred.

It is possible that Maslow's ideas referred to earlier, which were not put forward to help us understand industrial or organisational behaviour, have been asked to carry a greater weight of material than they were designed to bear. For example it is difficult to use Maslow's work to justify the assumption that fulfilment of higher order needs will lead to higher levels of productivity.

McGregor used Maslow's theory of hierarchy as a major part of his development of Theory X and Theory Y.[28] McGregor believed that management must provide the opportunity for people to satisfy their higher level needs at work. This is because better pay and conditions and improved security have removed the motivating effects of lower order needs. McGregor notes that, 'a satisfied need is not a motivator of behaviour'.[29]

Subsequent writers on motivation, however, have disagreed. In discussing what he calls ERG Theory, (standing for Existence, Relatedness and Growth), Alderfer suggests that,

'a satisfied need can remain a motivator ... if it is activated through serving as a substitute for some other need which itself is not being fully satisfied'.[30]

Alderfer's ERG Theory re-groups Maslow's seven major categories (allowing for the two subdivisions referred to above) into three and, more importantly, avoids the rigid premise that they constitute a hierarchy. He thus avoids the problem of what constitutes a 'satisfied' need or under what circumstances the hierarchy may be reversed. Rather he is able to develop a comprehensive set of propositions which relate to various conditions in the three need categories. While a number of these would be difficult to test, others hold some promise for a further application to the field of organisational behaviour. ERG Theory as developed by Alderfer asks questions of some of the conventional human relations' assumptions based on the Maslow hierarchy.

A further and better developed alternative to propositions based on Maslow's hierarchy is to be found in the ideas of 'expectancy theory' as put forward by Vroom and developed by Porter and Lawler.[31]

For our purposes, expectancy theory may be seen as having two main elements:

'What factors determine the *effort* a person puts into his job? What factors affect the relationship between effort and *performance*?'[32]

Effort, they suggest, is the product of two variables – the

Figure 4.2   Theoretical Model for Expectancy Theory

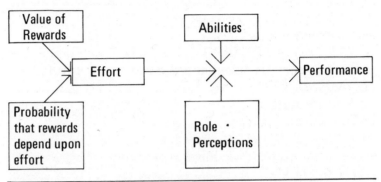

From E.E. Lawler III and L. Porter, 'Antecedent Attitudes of
Effective Managerial Performance', in V. Vroom and E. L. Deci,
Management and Motivation, Penguin Books
(Harmondsworth, 1970), p.256.

value of rewards and the perceived probability that rewards
depend upon effort. It is the changing nature of the former
and the subjective nature of the latter of these that is of
interest here. The authors note that,

> 'for any given individual at any particular point in
> time there is a variety of possible outcomes that he
> differentially desires'.[33]

While Maslow's hierarchy will subsume these outcomes and
while individuals have a relatively stable ordering of
rewards, 'values can and do change depending upon
various circumstances in the environment'.[34]

Having decided upon the rewards that he wishes to
pursue, the individual will perform in the way he personally
judges appropriate. The expenditure of effort in the pursuit

of rewards is thus a very subjective process, heavily dependent upon the individual's past experience and system of values.

Furthermore, actual performance, comprising effort and both ability and role perceptions, enters further subjective elements into the process.

While expectancy theory has raised a number of criticisms – for example that it assumes rational behaviour and ignores emotional responses – it usefully helps us to understand some of the research findings discussed earlier on direct participation.

We cannot assume that there is a single set of needs which serve to motivate. The things that motivate are to some extent the product of sub-parts of society and their special cultures and value systems. We have already suggested in the consideration of board level and middle range participation that models which work successfully in one society cannot be simply transposed to other countries irrespective of their culture and traditions. Similarly with direct participation we cannot assume that the values held in one culture, one country or one class will similarly determine goals and behaviour patterns elsewhere.

Kurt Lewin, for example, has written at length upon the cultural differences that existed between pre-Hitler Germany and America. At one point he discusses different attitudes to children in Germany and America:

'To one who comes from Germany, the degree of freedom and independence of children and adolescents in the United States is very impressive. Especially the lack of servility in the young child toward adults or of the student toward his professor is striking. The adults too treat the child much more on an equal footing whereas in Germany it seems to be the natural right of the adult to rule and the duty of the child to obey. The natural relation of adult and child is in the

United States not considered that of a superior (*Herr*) to
a subordinate (*Untergebener*) but that of two individuals
with the same right in principle.'[35]

Impressionistic evaluations of cultural differences should
always be treated with some caution but the point remains
that people's value systems do reflect their cultural
background. These value systems can be expected to
influence the responses that people make to schemes
designed to extend their ability to participate. This point
may be seen in the original experiments with the boys' club
in 1938. To what extent did the performance of the
democratic or participative group depend on the
democratic values prevalent in American culture? What
results would obtain if the experiment were repeated in
other cultures with more authoritarian or *laissez-faire*
traditions?

Similarly one might ask how far extensions of
participation in industry reflect a middle class system of
values and run counter to a working class system of
expectations of the managerial hierarchy. The findings of
Goldthorpe and his colleagues, for example, in their studies
in Luton suggest that the 'affluent worker' in their sample
had distinctively instrumental views of their work situation
which were part of the orientations which workers took
into the employment situation.[36]

The emphasis of such expectancy theory is thus on the
variability of motivations and role definitions among
workers. This variability has its origins outside the physical
limits of the factory or office. They lie in the orientations
that workers bring to their jobs from the wider social
context in which they live. Such orientations can be
expected to reflect the values prevalent in an individual's
family, in an individual's neighbourhood, in an individual's
school or church, trade union or occupation. Some
evidence has accumulated in the United States, for example,

which suggests that workers living in urban areas are less interested in the prospects of enlarged and enriched jobs and are more satisfied with repetitive work.[37] Blood and Hulin found, also in the United States, that the interest in job enrichment type programmes was strongly related to the nature of the community in which respondents lived.[38] Low interest in such programmes was noted in slum areas, in urban areas, and areas of high population density. Higher interest was noted in small, non-slum communities. This is not just a distinction between large and small communities but between communities with a range of different characteristics.

In summary it could be argued that the features of work which generate high levels of satisfaction vary from group to group. A middle class pattern emphasises variety, long time-spans of discretion, autonomy and low levels of repetition. The pattern characteristic of inner city slum areas or of large working class communities emphasises rather an instrumental set of satisfactions based on low levels of involvement and fairly repetitive work. This analysis leads to the suggestion that to impose middle class value systems on reluctant converts will not enhance job satisfaction, or the quality of life, or productivity. Rather it will be a wasteful exercise, not only detrimental to production, but distracting attention from the features of the work situation that need particular attention. These features would include arrangements for plant bargaining over such instrumental features as wages, bonuses, hours and conditions of work.

Such research and its implications should not be lightly dismissed. The success of direct participative programmes on green field sites away from hard core inner city areas, the success of such programmes in white collar activities or in specialist industries such as chemicals lend credibility to this position.

A counter position must be stated, however. Firstly, as

Daniel and McIntosh point out, there is no reason why we should expect workers to be entirely in favour of one value postion or another; workers may be interested in obtaining instrumental and expressive satisfaction. These authors suggest that 'the worker is interested in many different things in different contexts and circumstances', and they continue,

> 'in terms of understanding workers' behaviour and attitudes, the critical question is often not the one so frequently posed of *what* are people really interested or most interested in or *whether* they are more interested in job satisfaction and intrinsic rewards than money and extrinsic rewards, but rather, *when* are they interested in intrinsic rewards and *when* are they interested in extrinsic rewards'.[39]

A further point that may be usefully repeated here is the effect that general social changes are having on all our perceptions. Without denying the important sub-cultural variations that persist in the many communities of our complex industrial society, certain social changes are under way which will affect everyone to one degree or another. We have referred in this respect to changes in education, to changes in attitudes to authority, to the increased importance attaching to the enjoyment of life in all its aspects. These effects can be seen in the attitudes of students to their universities, of consumers to retailers and suppliers, of children to parents, of citizens to government departments, as well as of workers to management.

In the light of these various views on the applicability of participation to different groups, the manager might be expected to wonder whether he should bother at all. The theme that we are pursuing, however, is that different situations call for different approaches to participation. This will be developed in subsequent chapters when we discuss the implementation of whatever scheme is agreed. For the moment we may note the ideas of French and his colleagues, described in a study of participation in Norway.[40] They suggest that participation will only affect production, labour relations and job satisfaction to the extent that the following variables are present:[41]

1. the decisions with which participation is concerned are important;
2. the content of the decisions is relevant;
3. the participation is seen as legitimate;
4. there is no resistance to the methods of managing change.

This approach, they suggest, might explain 'differing effects of participation among different cultures, among different factories in the same culture and among individuals in the same factory'.

We shall now turn to a more detailed consideration of these differences and to their implications for the implementation of participation.

References

1. See R. White and R. Lippitt, *Autocracy and Democracy: An Experimental Enquiry*, Harper and Row (New York 1960).
2. K. Lewin, 'Group Decision and Social Change', in T.M. Newcombe and E.L. Hartley, *Readings in Social Psychology*, Henry Holt (New York 1953).
3. L. Coch and J.R.P. French Jr., 'Overcoming Resistance to Change', *Human Relations*, Vol 4, (1948), pp. 512–33.
4. *Ibid.*
5. A.H. Maslow, *Motivation and Personality*, Harper & Row (New York 1954).
6. *Ibid.*, p. 46.

7. *Ibid.*
8. M. Butteriss, *Job Enrichment and Employee Participation – A Study*, Institute of Personnel Management (London 1971), p. 35.
9. For a discussion of the different forms of job rotation see *Job Reform in Sweden*, Swedish Employers' Confederation (Stockholm, 1975), pp. 57–61.
10. *Ibid.*, pp. 53–5.
11. *Ibid.*
12. N.C. Morse and E. Reimer, 'The Experimental Change of a Major Organisational Variable', *Journal of Abnormal and Social Psychology* Vol 52, (1956), pp. 120–29.
13. *Ibid.*, p. 126.
14. *Ibid.*, p. 128.
15. *Ibid.*
16. R. Likert, *The Human Organisation*, McGraw-Hill (New York 1967).
17. W.S. Paul and K.B. Robertson, *Job Enrichment and Employee Motivation*, Gower Press (London 1971).
18. R.E. Walton, 'How to Counter Alienation in the Plant', *Harvard Business Review* (Nov-Dec. 1972), pp. 70–81.
19. *Ibid.*, p. 75.
20. For an account of these see *The Volvo Report*, Swedish Employers' Confederation (Stockholm 1975).
21. *Ibid.*, p. 26.
22. *Ibid.*, p. 74.
23. J. Edgren, *With Varying Success – A Swedish Experiment in Wage Systems and Shop Floor Organisation*, Swedish Employers' Confederation (Stockholm 1974).
24. G. Strauss, 'Participative Management: A Critique', *ILR Research*, Vol 12, (1966), pp. 3–6.
25. D. Katz, N. Maccoby, G. Gurin, L.G. Floor, *Productivity Supervision and Morale Among Railroad Workers*, Survey Research Center, Institute for Social Research, University of Michigan (Ann Arbor 1951); D. Katz, N. Maccoby, N.C. Morse, *Productivity, Supervision and*

Morale in an Office Situation, Survey Research Centre, Institute for Social Research, University of Michigan (Ann Arbor 1950).

26. D.C. Pelz, 'Influence: A Key to Effective Leadership in the First Line Supervisor', *Personnel*, Vol 29, (1952), pp. 209–17.

27. V. Vroom, *Work and Motivation*, John Wiley and Sons (New York 1964), pp. 181–6.

28. D. McGregor, *The Human Side of Enterprise*, McGraw-Hill (New York 1960).

29. *Ibid.*, p. 36.

30. C.P. Alderfer, *Existence, Relatedness, and Growth*, The Free Press (New York, 1972), p. 27.

31. E.E. Lawler III and L. Porter, 'Antecedent Attitudes of Effective Managerial Performance', in V. Vroom and E.L. Deci (Eds.), *Management and Motivation*, Penguin Books (Harmondsworth 1970).

32. *Ibid.*, p. 256.

33. *Ibid.*, p. 257.

34. *Ibid.*

35. K. Lewin, *Resolving Social Conflicts*, Souvenier Press (London 1973), pp. 6–7.

36. J.H. Goldthorpe, D. Lockwood, F. Bechhopper, J. Platt, *The Affluent Worker: Industrial Attitudes and Behaviour*, Cambridge University Press (Cambridge 1968).

37. A.N. Turner and P.R. Lawrence, *Industrial Jobs and the Worker*, Harvard University Press (Boston 1965).

38. M.R. Blood and C. Hulin, 'Alienation, Environmental Characteristics and Worker Responses', *Journal of Applied Psychology*, Vol. 51, (1967), pp. 284–90.

39. W.W. Daniel and N. McIntosh, *The Right to Manage?*, Macdonald (London 1972), p. 38.

40. J.R.P. French Jr., J. Israel, D.As, 'An Experiment on Participation in a Norwegian Factory', *Human Relations*, Vol. 13, (1960), pp. 3–19.

41. *Ibid.*, p. 17.

5 Putting participation in context

Introduction

Participation occurs in an organisational context which is a variable one. Organisations vary because they do different jobs, because different objectives underlie their work, and because their work is conducted in different settings or environments.

Organisations also share common characteristics. They will have, for example, some process of setting objectives, some means of monitoring progress and changing strategy and tactics, some means of collecting, channeling and evaluating information and some means of allocating and distributing rewards between different groups of organisational members. But while all organisations may share a need to complete some common tasks, the way in which they are completed and the priority which they are given will vary from situation to situation.

Organisations are to some extent able to control the ways in which they vary.* They can choose to manufacture or not manufacture products. They can choose to grow or stay at a given size. They can choose to adopt new techniques, to penetrate new markets, to acquire additional enterprises by take-over and merger.

---

* To talk of 'organisations controlling' is to use only a convenient shorthand for the fuller phrase 'people within organisations controlling'. Neither here nor elsewhere in this book should such phrases be taken to mean that organisations operate quite independently of the membership.

But organisations are not completely free in these respects. They contain skills and knowledge which predispose them to a particular product area and render difficult a quick and total switch. They may be required by statute to provide goods or services in a particular area. The decision not to grow may result in practice in contraction as competitors take advantage of potential orders and markets that might need to be turned down. They may need to adopt new techniques simply to remain competitive in terms of price, quality, product range or delivery time. This may in turn have implications for size, objectives or capital structure.

In other words, managers are only partly able to control their destiny. In many ways, the environment exerts pressures which cannot be ignored. The need to remain financially viable in a competitive world forces many companies to adopt practices they would ideally seek to avoid. To some extent environmental pressures are a force for conformity and similarity in organisational forms and processes. The trend to greater size, to more bureaucratisation, to increasing ratios of indirect administrative to direct production workers are examples of some common trends that may be noted. But environmental pressures impinge on firms differentially. Different products require different technologies and these, in turn, produce different organisational demands. Different markets have different features and these, in turn, have repercussions, not just for the organisation of sales, but for the entire company. Different patterns of ownership and control and different forms and intensity of competition add to the ways in which organisations in the private and the public sectors, and with profit-making and non-profit-making objectives, comprise quite different social systems which, while capable of comparison, are capable of generalisation at only quite low levels.

Organisations differ in at least three main ways. Firstly,

they differ in the kind of external environment which they confront. At its broadest level international comparisons might be made which examine the effects of different cultures, different social and legal systems and requirements or different industrial relations traditions. Within a particular country external environments of organisations also vary in the form of different markets, different raw material supplies and different subcultures from different regions providing their own distinctive industrial traditions.

Secondly, organisations also confront what we may call an internal environment. Although more susceptible to manipulation by the organisation, it may, as we suggested above, be determined by the choice (or imposition) of a particular product and the nature of the external environment. Elements which we would include in the internal environment include organisational size, organisational structure, technology and the tradition of industrial relations within the organisation. Under this heading would come also the prevailing attitudes and beliefs of groups at all levels within the company, the traditional values that pervade the company and such elements as the occupational structure and the system of rewards within the company.

The third way in which we suggest that organisations vary is in terms of organisational behaviour and performance. This includes characteristic forms of behaviour and performance both in terms of job performance by workers at all levels, and organisational performance measured against formally established criteria.

These three elements interact. Changes in any one part have implications for the other two. It is not a one-way process of influence, but a continuous process of interaction back and forth. Figure 5.1 gives a diagrammatic shape to our discussion. A detailed examination of all the factors involved here would be the subject of a book in its own right. In this chapter we will simply examine a small

Figure 5.1   Organisational Contexts

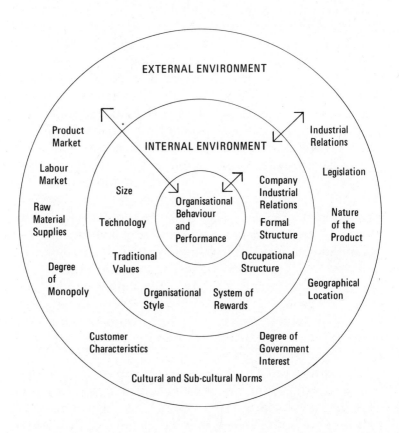

number of features which illustrate the ways in which the practice of participation, far from being an independent factor which may be injected into organisations at will, is a highly variable concept which will be adopted in different forms and at different speeds by organisations seeking to modify behaviour and performance.

Products and markets

It may be thought that, in their ability to choose the 'business they are in', managers are free to influence a great part of their environment. However, as we have suggested above, this freedom may be difficult to realise. Many public bodies have their 'business' defined for them. Educational bodies, health authorities, penal institutions, local government cannot decide to cease traditional operations and get into more profitable or less troublesome lines. Nationalised industries, likewise, have little room for manoeuvre in their product area. Voluntary associations owe their entire *raison d'etre* to a single 'product line'. Charities, for example, can hardly abandon their cause in order to seek operations in a 'softer' environment.

Private firms have other constraints. A great deal of their capital lies in their knowledge of a particular product. Their labour force may have specific skills in handling particular raw materials or completing particular work processes. The sales and marketing team will have a knowledge of the market and a range of contacts which have been painstakingly established. Other members of the management team, in purchasing, production, or research and development, for example, will have similar knowledge and abilities which comprise the social assets of the firm. Such factors not only make it difficult for managers to imagine moving out of their traditional product area, it makes so doing a costly operation.

But operations in a particular product area have implications for the remainder of the business and determine in large part the remaining environmental factors. The most directly affected will be the nature of the market and the nature of the production process.

A key factor in the nature of the product and its associated markets and technology, is the degree of stability. Several writers have pointed to the ways in which firms in different product areas have experienced different rates of change. Burns and Stalker[1] examined firms in the textiles and electronics industries, for example, and came to certain conclusions about their respective rates of change and the implications of these differential rates of change for management and organisation. They also noted that pre-existing styles of management had implications for the speed and efficacy with which change would be implemented.

Burns and Stalker suggest that organisations may be described as lying between two extremes which they call the mechanistic and the organic. Organisations enjoying more stability in their environments – in their technology, in their product range, in their markets – would normally be found towards the mechanistic end of the continuum. Those organisations with lower levels of stability, with higher levels of uncertainty in the areas we have mentioned, would more appropriately be placed towards the organic end of the continuum. This proposition is of considerable interest for our discussion of participation. The characteristics of mechanistic and organic types described by Burns and Stalker reveal organisations which are peculiarly receptive to the development of participation or which are likely to produce stern resistance. For example, they include in their description of the mechanistic system an emphasis on individual tasks, on the location of ultimate knowledge at the top of the hierarchy, and on the hierarchical nature of control, authority and communications. These are precisely the characteristics that participative management reverses. Emphasis is now placed in varying degrees on the extension of individual tasks and the development of group tasks. The belief underlying participation is that useful contributions to the pursuit of organisational objectives may be found at any point in the organisational hierarchy and the purpose of participative management styles is to release that potential in the interests of the organisation as a whole. A continual emphasis on hierarchy, on vertical relationships, on one-to-one reporting up the line provides no opportunity for contribuitons to be made by people not organisationally defined as having a contribution to make on a specific issue.

These facilities for participation, however, appear strongly in Burns and Stalker's description of the organic system. Emphasis here is placed on 'the contributive nature of special knowledge and experience to the common task of the concern' and 'the spread of commitment to the concern beyond any technical definition'. The organic type of organisation is characterised, not by a hierarchy of relationships but by a network, not by an omniscient head but by an awareness that persons throughout the organisation and irrespective of their formal level, may have special knowledge that contributes to the solution of a particular problem or class of problems.

One can see the ways in which these alternative management systems are appropriate to the respective conditions of certainty and uncertainty arising from the nature of the product. Where little change has been experienced after a long period, there is little incentive for managers to seek contributions from unusual sources within the hierarchy. The problems are known; the solutions well-tried and modified through practice. Uncertainty and change, however, may make these well-tried solutions inappropriate and give rise to a need, not just for new solutions to new problems but for new ways of achieving such solutions.

This leads us to what is perhaps the major contribution of the mechanistic-organic continuum to our thinking about participation. The operation of an organic system requires, not just a series of structural organisational characteristics but rather a distinctive management style. Such a style will ensure that appropriate responses are made to the demands of high levels of uncertainty in the environment. The absence of such a style makes it difficult for managers to respond in a receptive way to the ideas of people at lower levels in the organisation. There is no guarantee that environmental pressure for a participative style will produce an appropriate style. Managers who have lived with change and participation in the past may readily continue with such a style in the future. Managers who have appropriately confronted essentially stable situations in the past may find it much harder to adapt to the new demands of uncertainty.

A further difficulty with the concept of mechanistic and organic management styles is that a single organisation will include departments or divisions which vary between themselves in the extent to which one style or another is predominant. The management task of co-ordination is not simply a matter of bringing together different departmental activities to meet organsiational objectives. It is also a problem of bringing together into a single co-operative system, managers with different attitudes and styles.[2] Marketing attracts and needs managers with a particular style. Research and development, accountancy, production engineering, data processing – each has a stereotyped style. Such stereotypes disguise as much as they reveal. But they underline the fact that differences do exist in the typical age, educational background, careers and aspirations of managers in different disciplines. These differences are a frequent source of friction in organisational relationships, and are part of the much discussed staff-line problem.[3]

They are likely to be matched by differences of attitude to participation. Participative styles will flourish in some departments and divisions; it will always be an up-hill struggle in other parts of the organisation. Where participation is the official company 'line' the non-participating groups will be out of sympathy with the remainder. In autocratic organisations, departments predisposed to participation will find their relationships outside the department a source of strain.

As Hebden and his colleagues found in their study of computerisation,[4] the data processing (d.p.) department can be a source of such discontinuities in management style. The participative style adopted by the d.p. department in Hebden's plant A jarred not only with the bureaucratic style in the surrounding production departments, but with the bureaucratic style of the accountant and his department to whom d.p. was formally responsible. Data processing was thus isolated in terms of its style and ability to communicate with others, both laterally from other departments, and vertically from the sources of power in the firm.

For managers wishing to extend, not computerised systems, but a participative style of management, such discontinuities can provide an insurmountable obstacle. They will certainly reduce the effectiveness of the total participative effort and prevent the achievement of the interrelated system proposed here.

Such aspects of an organisation's external environment are applicable not only to industrial or commercial organisations. The same concepts apply to such apparently dissimilar organisations as schools and universities, hospitals and social service organisations, local government and departments of the civil service. Members of these organisations may not think of themselves as dealing with 'a product' or entering 'a market', but they are in practice engaging in transactions with the bigger world outside their own organisation. These transactions take place, depending on the organisation's objectives and area of activity, in conditions of greater or lesser stability and certainty. This affects the attitudes of the members. Such organisations will also contain groups differentially pre-disposed to participation by virtue of their daily tasks and problems and, as in industry, this will influence the form that implementation must take.

We have discussed only products and markets. As we suggest in Figure 5.1 there are many other elements in the external environment. Discussion could continue, for example, about the implications for organisations (and, therefore, for participation) of government actions, trade union actions in the industry generally, the nature of the labour market or of the raw materials market. All these impact themselves on management with different degrees of force. They promote to differing extents a need for preparedness to change which will colour attitudes to participation and affect the strategy needed for its introduction.

Technology

As with the elements of the external environment, elements of the internal environment also hold implications for the introduction and operation of participation. These implications lie in the direct limitations that size and technology impose on the practice of participation and, more indirectly, in the generation of attitudes towards participation and expectations of what participation can achieve.

The relationship between technology and organisational behaviour has been examined by many authors. The usual approach to technology has been to envisage a chronological development in which the mode of production moves from individual craft production through a range of small batch and large batch production methods to the situation of mass production with assembly line techniques. The continuum is then extended to more completely automated and process flow situations. Joan Woodward[5] in her analysis of the relationship between management organisation and technology identified eleven different production systems in South Essex industry ranging from 'production of units to customers' requirements' to 'continuous flow production of liquids, gases and crystalline substances' and also including some systems which combined more than one of the technology stages.

Woodward found relationships between various organisational characteristics and technology among firms with a more than average level of commercial success. These organisational characteristics included, for example, the number of levels in the hierarchy, the spans of control of such people as the chief executives or first line supervision, the ratio of direct to indirect workers, the emphasis on written communication and the extent to which duties and responsibilities were clearly defined.

Woodward's conclusion that there was a link between 'technology, organisation and performance', that 'there was a particular form of organisation most appropriate to each technical situation',[6] is particularly relevant to our discussion of the different situations in which participation may be tried. Specifically, Woodward reports that successful organisations at either end of her spectrum of technology – which for convenience we will call unit and process production – are characterised by small primary working groups engendering informal and intimate relationships between supervisor and worker. Occupational structure also varied with technology, and unit and process production systems involved higher proportions of skilled workers than the mass production situation.

Also important for our discussion of participation, organisations at either end of the continuum tended to an organic management system while those in the middle range were more mechanistic. Firms in unit and process production were more flexible, with less emphasis on formal rights and obligations.

Similar findings have been reported by other researchers. We have already noted the work of Burns and Stalker. Studies of individual plants by industrial sociologists lend further credence to the description that Woodward gives of different technologies.[7] Perhaps the most systematic confirmation of Woodward's position is offered by Robert Blauner.[8] Taking a similar technological spectrum, he notes that levels of alienation among manual workers are at their lowest at either end of the continuum. Blauner suggests that the degree of meaning in work, and control over the work situation, the level of social integration and of self-fulfilment all reach their nadir with mass production techniques. Woodward notes that this form of production places the greatest pressure on managers and supervisors and promotes high levels of tension throughout the organisation.

The implication of these studies for our discussion of participation is paradoxical. Left alone, the forces of technology seem likely to promote more organic and participative structures at either end of the technological spectrum. Smaller groups of skilled workers, a more relaxed atmosphere, a closer relationship between workers and supervisors, provide conditions under which participation is more easily introduced. The expectations and indeed the existing practices favour participation. They produce what we have noted French and his colleagues[9] call a *legitimacy* for participation. Participation is seen by the parties involved as the 'right and proper' way to operate.

The different technologies with which different firms operate impinge on the legitimacy with which participation is judged. They also impinge on the perceived relevance of participation. Participation is pointless in situations where the important decisions are already seen to have been pre-empted by the demands of the technology itself. The irony is that in situations where participation is most evidently needed – to alleviate what Blauner describes as the alienating by-product of mass production technology – it may be most difficult to implement. Where it is most readily acceptable, the urgency surrounding its implementation is less acute.

Again, as with our discussion of the external environment, we should recognise that a single technology may not be found throughout the firm. It is often the case that where many technologies coexist one particular technology may dominate, possibly because of its primary importance in the organisation, possibly because of the power exercised in the organisation by those associated with it. But we should also recognise that organisations employing several different technologies will have sub-parts in varying degrees of readiness and receptivity to the introduction of participation. This can create the problems for participation and for interaction between departments with different participative practices which we referred to above.

A further question now arises. If Woodward's findings are correct and successful organisations in some technolgies operate with less participative styles, should we not be wary of seeking to make all organisations, irrespective of their situation, equally participative? It might be argued that as technologies – unit, mass or process – will be associated with particular structures and behaviour patterns, there is little point in attempting to introduce such alternative patterns as those associated with participative management and described in Chapter 4. If this is inappropriate to the technological situation of the firm, such innovations will at best be rejected as irrelevant by those required to work them and, more seriously, may lead the organisation along such a dangerous and inappropriate path as to jeopardise the effectiveness and ultimately the survival of the firm. As Woodward has noted, the firms enjoying an above average success engaged in organisational practices 'normal' for firms in that technology. Firms that deviated from the norm tended to be less effective in their pursuit of commercial success. Given this perspective, it might be argued that firms should give technology its head, pursue appropriate forms for business success, and accept the consequences as part of the price of being in business.

Neither Woodward nor Blauner, however, commit themselves to such a totally fatalistic view of the course and destiny of business organisation. Blauner notes at the outset

that his 'study does not follow a totally deterministic
approach. In certain situations, the conscious organisational
policies of industrial management may be critical in their
effects on employee alienation.'[10]

If this is so, then the ability of management to rise above
the constraints of its technology may be an important
element in the variable organisational performance that
Woodward's own figures reveal both among firms which
approximate to the organisational norm and those whose
structures deviate.

While the main-stream of both Blauner's and
Woodward's theses suggests that relationships at work are
centrally formed by technology, a close examination of
their work shows that this is not inevitably so. Alternative
organisational forms can be successful within a single
technology. Alternative behavioural patterns can arise
within a single technology. Equally, alternative technologies
can be developed to allow for different organisational forms
and to encourage different patterns of organisational
behaviour. These two possibilities may be discussed in turn.

The idea that work involves a combination of both social
organisation and technical aspects has only been recognised
during the post-war years. This theme received special
impetus from the work of the Tavistock Institute with the
coinage of the term 'socio-technical system'. Previous
writers had sought improvements in organisational
effectiveness by concentration on the purely technical
aspects of work without consideration of the social (or
human) element. Typical of this approach had been the pre-
war advocates of Scientific Management.[11] Equally one-
sided had been the original Human Relations researchers,
who, in their attempt to redress the balance against
Scientific Management, emphasised the social nature of the
work situation with little reference to the technical context.

Nevertheless the effect of these early Human Relations
experiments was to demonstrate that even with technology

held constant, different attitudes and behaviour patterns could be obtained from workers by introducing different managerial styles and encouraging different forms of social organisation among workers.[12]

In the original Hawthorne experiments, for example, Mayo found that without any major change in the technology, new kinds of relationship between supervisors and workers were associated with increased output. Roethlisberger and Dickson note that while 'the minor alterations in method of assembly operation seemed to be insignificant'[13] there was a 'gradual change in social inter-relationship among operators themselves' and 'a change in the relation between operators and their supervisors'.[14] These authors conclude that, in a situation where technology was held constant, increases in output were due primarily to changing social circumstances.

A quarter of a century later in the very different circumstances of the Durham coal fields, the possibilities inherent in variable forms of social organisation within a constant technology were again demonstrated. Trist and Bamforth[15] showed how a change in technology from a hand-got method had resulted in the destruction of pre-existing social groups and their norms and values.

The hand-got method was characterised by multi-skilled groups capable of carrying out a range of tasks that the group might encounter. Isolated in the pit, the group had high levels of discretion in establishing its work programme. The new longwall method introduced specialisation by shift. Each shift was given its own range of work and trained specifically in that work. The sequence of shifts ensures that the total range of necessary tasks is completed. The system, however, generated dissatisfaction within the shift groups and conflict between the shifts. Problems and bad work were conveniently blamed on other shifts and they elevated their own shift above the total objectives.

Changes in social organisation within the prevailing technology improved this situation. A 'composite' longwall system was introduced. Emphasis was placed on the common task and shift groups were made to encompass several skills. The work cycle was taken as far as possible on each shift and picked up by successive shifts wherever the previous shifts had left off. The point we wish to emphasise here is that within a single technology, forms of social organisation were possible which maximised or minimised the participation possible by the group in organising the work.

Such reorganisation within the technology may not be successfully achieved at the first attempt. The Swedish Employers Confederation cite the re-organisation of a Swedish ship-yard.[16] The principle used here was that versatile multi-skilled units should be responsible for entire deck-sections. Accordingly, old occupational groupings of electricians, carpenters, painters, etc., were re-allocated to the new units. It became apparent that such occupational group members resented the isolation from their colleagues that the new system engendered. The system was further re-organised on a matrix basis so that every individual belonged both to deck-section units and to occupational groups. This system produced satisfactory results. The example demonstrates again that, without changing technology, it is possible to obtain a variety of forms of social organisation. Further examples of this were described in the last chapter.

We also discussed in Chapter 4 the opposite position. Several organisations have now achieved improvements in participation by introducing new forms of social organisation within alternative technologies. In addition to the revolutionary Volvo plant at Kalmar, a similar experimental factory has been built by Saab-Scania to accommodate their Saab 99 engine production at Södertälje.[17] Both these projects demonstrate the feasibility of changing the dominant technology to facilitate new forms of social organisation and increased levels of direct participation. Both these projects await the judgment of the market place.

The form of technology that may be found in a company, is an important element in establishing that organisation's starting point for the long haul to participation. Technology, however, should not be regarded as the determining factor, deciding whether participation is possible at all. Certain technologies, craft and unit technologies for example, are associated with relatively small scale operations and these two factors may work together in making participation more readily obtainable. Process technology, although associated with large capital investment and large scale operations, may nevertheless be characterised by a relatively small labour force and small self-contained groups. This feature, together with the different kinds of pressure and the greater discretion in freedom obtaining in process plants may similarly pre-dispose the organisation to a participative style of supervision and management. But these technologies will not of themselves generate participative management; nor does the prevalence of mass assembly technology within an organisation preclude that organisation from developing participative forms. Management in the latter situation may have to think more creatively to design workable schemes of participation. They may need to be more tolerant in accepting false starts, reversals, criticism and cynicism in the process of building for participation. They may have to work at the business of maintaining participation. We should recognise the handicaps to participation that exist from the outset and in particular the need to establish among all parties the legitimacy of participation. But such handicaps can be overcome if the will to make paricipation succeed is present at the most senior levels and is imparted to others at each level within the organisation.

Organisational size and structure

The reference to organisational size in the preceding paragraphs may now be discussed in some detail for size is a key variable affecting the nature of inter-personal relationships and differentiating organisations which seek to introduce greater degree of participation.

Although any examination of the distinctive features of organisations must include a consideration of size, it becomes an issue for participation when certain minimum thresholds are passed. While it is not possible to stipulate as a universal rule where these thresholds will be – it clearly depends on the various other aspects which differentiate organisations – we can note the features of large scale organisation which give rise to demands for more participation.

The growth of organisations will take a variety of forms depending upon the exact context within which it operates. To achieve growth, however, certain organisational mechanisms are likely to be employed. The first of these we might call specialisation. To achieve increased output the one man business or the small partnership will need to employ increased numbers in such specialist task areas as production, sales, purchasing, accounts etc.[18] While the application of specialisation can bring enormous benefits in growth terms, these will be 'paid' for through new problems as the firm grapples with the quite new issues of achieving co-ordination and control, of maintaining communications and commitment among increasingly disparate groups.

One means of resolving some of these problems and of dealing with the increased spans of control that organisational growth gives rise to is the provision of additional hierarchical levels.

Large organisations, characterised by the application of principles of specialisation and hierarchy, resolve the problems of co-ordination and communication at one level, only to see them reappear at a different level and in a different form. The needs that organisations have to achieve predictability and uniformity in their operations ultimately give rise to a formalisation of procedures, to impersonal criteria and decision rules. The acceptance and implementation of such bureaucratic paraphernalia similarly give rise to the possibility of rigidity, of a preoccupation with means rather than ends and a new ethic pervading the organisation which emphasises a 'safe' solution to problems rather than a bold or entrepreneurial venture.

It is these pathological aspects of large scale organisation that have prompted many behavioural scientists to seek alternative forms of administration of large scale enterprise and even to predict the ultimate demise of bureaucracy. As Bennis noted,

'in the next twenty-five to fifty years ... we should witness and participate in the end of bureaucracy as we know it and the rise of the new social systems better suited to twentieth-century demands of industrialisation'.[19]

The organisational forms that will replace bureaucracy invariably involve some form of participative management. What has not been demonstrated, however, is whether size, the feature that more than any other gave rise to bureaucracy, can be managed by non-bureaucratic forms.

The issue here is similar to that discussed in relation to technology. *De facto* participation occurs without conscious planning in small organisations. In larger units, where participation might be a useful alternative to bureaucracy, it is most difficult to obtain. The entire training, background and experience of the parties involved militate against participation. The imposition of participation by establishing its forms and trappings will not legitimise it in the eyes of those who expect different kinds of relationships between managers and managed. But this is often the bureaucratic response to a sensed need to break with bureaucratic forms. A recent research report by Opinion Research Centre,[20] for example, showed that large companies were more likely to have formal schemes of participation such as a works council or other joint committee where selected employees meet the management. In a random sample of over 2000 respondents, fifty-nine per cent of those employed in large companies reported the existence of such a committee compared with only twenty-four per cent in the small companies. The smaller companies, however, had a slight edge in the satisfaction of workers with such schemes. Seventy-eight per cent of respondents in small companies reported positively compared with seventy-three per cent in large companies and sixty-seven per cent in multinational companies.

In small organisations, formal schemes of participation are pre-empted by a greater sense of participation which pervades the company. Ingham, for example, has described the different kinds of communication patterns that he found in a range of companies of different sizes.[21]

As is shown in Tables 5.1 and 5.2, reproduced from Ingham, workers in small firms are much more likely to enter into direct interaction with works management and with directors than are their equals in large companies. Given the frequency of such interaction in small firms, the need for formal schemes of participation may be less urgent. In large organisations, where communications between different levels in the hierarchy may be less frequent, participation may serve a useful function in augmenting such communication.[22]

However, this may not be easy to achieve. Workers in large and small organisations may also differ from each

Table 5.1 Direct interaction with shop supervisor/works manager by organisation and skill level

	Small firms		Large plant A		Large plant B
	Unit & Small-batch technology		Unit & small-batch technology		Mass production technology
	Semi-skilled	Skilled	Semi-skilled	Skilled	Semi-skilled
Talk to shop supervisor/ works manager	100 %	100 %	45 %	39 %	35 %
Do *not* talk to shop supervisor/ works manager	0 %	0 %	55 %	61 %	65 %
Total %	100 %	100 %	100 %	100 %	100 %
N	14	20	20	26	23

G.K. Ingham, *Size of Industrial Organisation and Worker Behaviour*, Cambridge University Press (Cambridge 1970), Table 7.1, p. 73.

other in the extent to which they want to be involved in closer communications with higher levels of management. Referring again to Ingham's work, when workers were asked what were the most important considerations in their job choice, between fifty-four per cent and seventy-four per cent of those in large firms mentioned economic considerations alone compared with between four per cent and nine per cent in small firms. By contrast, between thirty-two per cent and forty per cent of workers in small

Table 5.2 Direct interaction with director by size of organisation and skill level

	Small firms		Large plant A		Large plant B
	Unit & small-batch technology		Unit & small-batch technology		Mass production technology
	Semi-skilled	Skilled	Semi-skilled	Skilled	Semi-skilled
Talk to director	95 %	96 %	0 %	4 %	0 %
Do *not* talk to director	5 %	4 %	100 %	96 %	100 %
Total %	100 %	100 %	100 %	100 %	100 %
N	22	25	20	26	23

G.K. Ingham, *Ibid*, Table 7.3, p. 75.

firms referred to non-economic considerations alone compared with between nil and eight per cent in large firms.[23] Non-economic considerations include such things as interesting work, good social relationships and certain physical attributes of work. Within these categories, no one in the large firms referred to the value of friendly relationships.

The value of establishing one's objectives in developing participation may now be seen more clearly. Participation which seeks simply to develop the loyalty of workers to the firm or provide more satisfying social relationships between men and management will succeed most readily in those small organisations where workers are already pre-disposed to place a high value on close personal relationships with more senior staff.

In large organisations, workers are more likely to be indifferent to the presence of absence of such relationships. It may be that the frequency (or infrequency) of these relationships affects the views of those involved after they have joined the company. But there does seem to be some evidence that people choose to work in large firms with a particular set of considerations in mind. These exclude a high value on informal and friendly relationships with superiors.

If this is so, is there any point in developing participation in small firms in order to reinforce what is already working well by other means? Is there any value in large firms developing among workers something which they may have explicitly rejected by choosing to work where they have? Participation which seeks to promote improved worker-management relationships will succeed most readily in those organisations where high trust already exists. It cannot be introduced elsewhere by fiat and bureaucratic procedures. If it is to work at all, in large or small organisations, it will be through the patient building of relationships based on trust.

Participation may be said to have succeeded in organisations of all sizes when, through the development of such relationships, individuals are free to express their views and opinions about their work and such expressions are taken seriously and acted upon by colleagues and superiors. In a perhaps hackneyed phrase, participation is thus about improved communications. Communications became meaningful, not only when people are prepared to listen, but when people are free and feel free to talk. When participation is working, it is making available to the total organisation a large potential of knowledge and experience of the firm's operations from people at all levels which is denied to the firm that is unable to involve its members in a constructive dialogue with each other.

The cost of impersonal relationships in large, bureaucratically organised enterprises is not the loss of a friendly atmosphere. It is rather when there is a resulting failure by the respective parties to pool their knowledge to further organisational objectives. The development of social and organisational distance and boundaries renders more easy the development of sub-group goals at odds with ultimate organisational goals. This does not imply however that high levels of interaction between various groupings in small organisations result necessarily in the more effective pursuit of organisational goals.

A major purpose of participation in small organisations must be to build upon and develop the informal relationships that exist between workers and management in the interests of greater total effectiveness. If this is not done, the social capital represented by these relationships will remain simply as a reservoir of goodwill. Conscious development of participation seeks to use and develop the social capital.

The purpose of participation in the large organisation is not to develop a new quality in social relationships against the wishes of workers who have chosen to work in that firm. A major purpose is rather to ensure that, despite an absence of such relationships, the special knowledge and experience of workers at all levels and in all kinds of positions within the organisation may be deployed in the interests of the total organisation's effectiveness.

Occupational structure and industrial relations

The growth of organisation, the development of technology and of specialisation bring subsequent development in the occupational structure of the organisation. Many attempts have been made to produce a classification of occupations and these have now reached levels of minute detail and enormous refinement.[24] More helpful for our purpose is the seven-point division referred to by W. H. Scott and his colleagues.[25] This consisted of:

1. professional
2. managerial
3. supervisory and technical
4. clerical
5. skilled manual
6. semi-skilled manual
7. unskilled manual.

Although over twenty years old, this classification remains applicable today. The different elements in the classification are self-explanatory. We should note that organisations will vary in the extent to which these elements are present, and in the relative power accruing to each.

But the importance for participation stems only partly from the classification *per se*; also important is a consideration of the elements of the classification as occupational groups. An occupational group comprises people who share a common task or interrelated set of tasks and who share 'certain common values, attitudes, interests and patterns of behaviour'.[26] Occupational structure holds implications for behaviour and for participation to the extent that the membership identify with their respective occupational interests. Some parts of the above classification can be more readily described as occupational groups in the way that we have defined them than others. Some of the categories do not contain occupational groups in that the membership do not identify with each other, do not share the necessary common values and attitudes. Such people may hold instead an organisational identification or may be quite instrumental in their views of work and hold no particular identification.

Groups which hold a strong occupational identification have probably undergone a lengthy period of occupational training and hold membership of an occupational organisation such as a professional association or trade union which is beyond the confines of the employing organisation.[28] Of course groups without strong occupational commitments may also be members of trade unions but we suggest that the meaning such membership holds for them will be different. It may, for example, be for instrumental, rather than expressive purposes.

The pattern of occupational groups with their varying levels of identification with occupation or employer will both reflect and hold implications for the tradition of industrial relations within a particular organisation. Is the organisation characterised predominantly by white collar clerical tasks with low levels of unionisation and high levels of organisational identification even to the extent of internal company unions? Does the organisation employ significant numbers of professional or technical staff with a commitment to the task that goes beyond any organisational deefinition of rights and duties? Does the organisation predominantly employ semi-skilled or unskilled workers seeing neither an identification with their occupation nor with their employing organisation but rather enjoying an instrumental view of work and committed only to optimising such instrumental returns?

Different occupational groups will have different patterns of organisation, different interests to pursue and protect, and different contexts in which to operate which render them more or less amenable to processes of participation involving some degree of acceptance of a total organisational perspective. The occupational structure of a company is an important variable affecting the kinds of issues with which industrial relations activity has been concerned and affecting the ways in which these issues have been pursued. Individual occupational groups will carry an industrial relations tradition which cannot be ignored but which will affect the ease with which participation may be implemented. The varying traditions, for example, of coal miners, dockers and railway engine drivers are too obvious to need elaboration. But all companies contain some form of occupational structure and management should be sensitive to the implications of the particular structure for their specific ambitions with regard to participation.

This point may be expanded to a broader consideration of the implications of the industrial relations situations more generally for the implementation and practice of participation. The part of industrial relations will be affected by each of the factors discussed in this chapter – by the nature of the product and its markets, by the technology and by the size and structure of the organisation. It will also be influenced by the attitudes of the parties involved – of management and unions, of shop stewards, foremen and workers – and these attitudes are in part the result of the variables· described above. But they are also in part the product of a more intangible tradition and system of values which differentiate one plant from another.

Paternalistic and autocratic, family or managerially dominated, employee centred or concerned with short-term economic gains – organisations enjoy a reputation with their employeees, their customers and suppliers, and in the community at large. The traditional values that permeate an organisation may have little basis in fact. They may result from a smaller number of incidents which have developed in the 'collective memory' we call tradition but which now influence behaviour. In the words of the sociologist W. I. Thomas, 'if men define situations as real, they are real in their consequences'. Irrespective of the accuracy of men's views of their employer, they will act on the strength of what they believe to be true.

In approaching an extension of participation, management will need to operate within the confines of such a tradition or legacy of industrial relations. Some firms will thus start with an advantage. Their occupational structure may foster a sense of identification with the task or with the organisation itself. Their record of industrial relations may, in the eyes of the participants, be a good one.

There will be no legacy of bad-feeling and mistrust to be overcome. Elsewhere the history of industrial relations may be perceived as bad. Management-labour or inter-occupational disputes may have erected traditional barriers to communication and co-operation which the men involved cannot easily overcome. Any extension of participation takes place in an organisational setting which is not just the product of a set of objectively assessable factors such as technology or product market variations. Each unique organisational setting is also the product of its history, of events long passed and of the way memories of such events are recorded and cherished by those who are now expected to become participants in the new organisational style of the future. It is not possible to separate the future from the past. The two are linked in the memories and perceptions of the individuals and groups involved.

Conclusions

The purpose of this chapter has been to show some of the ways in which organisations may vary and to begin a discussion of the implications that such variations hold for the implementation and practice of participation. Two levels of variable factors have been elaborated – the external environment and the internal environment.

The external environment contains elements over which individual managers, once committed to particular objectives, have little or no control. We would include here broad cultural features of the countries in which they operate, sub-cultural features of particular regions, conurbations or cities. We have discussed in more detail such features of the external environment as the nature of the product market and the amount of uncertainty that some market forms can generate with important ramifications on managerial attitudes.

This same concern with levels of uncertainty and managerial ability to confront change emerged from our discussion of certain parts of what we called the internal environment. Technology, we have suggested, is important not only for the physical constraints it imposes on one form of participation or another – indeed, given the will, such constraints are only rarely a complete obstacle. Technology is significant for the conduct of participation because of the way it affects attitudes and accepted ways of behaving. Formal organization similarly varies through degrees of bureaucratisation in the extent to which managers normally confront relative stability, in which their problems are essentially repeats of yesterday's experience, in which problem solving involves not creative innovation but a search of previous approaches to a similar situation.

Participation, we have already suggested, cannot be confined to one part of the organisation or to one level of decision. Participation we would now add, cannot be implemented simply as a mechanistic bringing together of appropriate institutions. For these institutions to work, life must be breathed into them by the actions of the membership. This will only happen if the membership believe in the process.

In the authors' experience, many companies can be usefully understood in terms of the variables discussed in this chapter. The situation is complicated, however, in the case of multi-product companies. Here a range of products takes the company into many markets and technologies, involves many different manufacturing facilities in different countries and different regions within countries. The company may comprise units of different size, with different structures and with different industrial relations traditions.

Many such companies find that these 'dissimilarities' from one part to another lead to a need for decentralisation. The decentralised operations may then be understood in terms of the variables we have discussed and their implications for participation considered de-centralised company by de-centralised company.

The situation is complicated when there is a smaller degree of de-centralisation and companies seek to develop participation in a common way under the different circumstances of separate divisions.

One company encountered by the authors was in freight transport and distribution. This involved the company in many different kinds of operation. It was active in shipping, air freight and road transport. These activities had led to further interests in lighterage and towage, warehousing and container repair.

Each of these activities had its own distinctive problems and traditions. It is not simply the obvious differences in technology to which we are drawing attention here. Rather we would emphasise the way in which the company was involved in a range of external and internal environments. Air and sea freight, for example, differ not just in the obvious physical differences but in such other areas as the speed of turn-round, in terms of the rate of change and in terms of the strength of tradition. The pressures of the market are different. The sizes of the 'production units' are different. The legal frameworks in which they operate are different. Even within a single operation major differences could be found. In road haulage, for example, local delivery arrangements and trans-European road freight involved different kinds of labour forces with different values and traditions and expectations.

Organizing for their many different operations involved the company in understanding quite different social systems. In approaching participation these different social systems needed to be penetrated appropriately for participation to be either technically feasible or seen as legitimate by the membership. Organising for participation brings different problems on board ship, in the trans-continental juggernaut lorry and in the regional warehouse depot. These occupational groups also believed in participation in varying degrees.

The company had developed a philosophy of participation but it faced the problem of the differential speed with which it could be implemented in its different operations. To some extent the situation was eased by the great dispersion of the employees and the reduced likelihood of invidious comparisons. Furthermore each major activity had a separate identity which permitted different practices to be followed appropriately in different situations.

Nevertheless the company wished to pursue its philosophy throughout its operations. Comparisons from company to company could be made by groups of employees who were adjacent and by trade unionists who saw more of the total picture. The company has tried to avoid a 'credibility-gap' between its espoused and well-publicised philosophy and differential rates of practical implementation by establishing targets and calling for regular progress reports on specified dates towards such targets. The company thus avoids laying down a rigid pattern for progress to participation which would be inapplicable in many cases; but it also avoids the dangers flowing from 'holes' in the fabric and the subsequent charges of hyprocrisy, by having a philosophy, an overall sense of direction and a systematic programme of review and report.

Participation does not occur in a vacuum. It is implemented in a pre-existing social system and attitudes towards such an innovation will necessarily be coloured by the institutions and experience of that pre-existing social system. The social system of the organisation conditions the expectations of all the participants and limits the extent to which participation is deemed 'legitimate' or 'relevant' by the various parties. A great part of the implementation process, once the decision for greater participation has been taken, is concerned with the adaptation of the social system so that it is not incompatible with the demands of participation. It is to this process of implementation that we now turn.

References

1. T. Burns and G.M. Stalker, *The Management of Innovation*, Tavistock Publications (London 1961).
2. This theme is explored in detail by P.R. Lawrence and J.W. Lorsch, *Organisation and Environment*, Harvard University (Cambridge 1967).
3. For a development of this, see M. Dalton, *Men Who Manage*, Wiley and Sons, (New York 1959).
4. J.E. Hebden, M.J. Rose, W.H. Scott, 'Management Structure and Computerisation', *Sociology*, Vol 3, (Sept. 1969), pp. 377–96.
5. J. Woodward, *Industrial Organisation: Theory and Practice*, Oxford University Press (London 1965).
6. *Ibid.*, p. 72.
7. For example C.R. Walker and R.H. Guest, *Man on the Assembly Line*, Yale University Press (New Haven 1957); H. Beynon, *Working for Ford*, Penguin Books (Harmondsworth 1973).
8. R. Blauner, *Alienation and Freedom*, University of Chicago Press (Chicago 1964).
9. J.R.P. French, J. Israel and D.Äs, 'An Experiment on Participation in a Norwegian Factory', *Human Relations*, Vol 19 (1960), pp. 3–19.
10. Blauner, *op. cit.*, p. 11.
11. F.W. Taylor, *The Principles of Scientific Management*, Harper and Row (New York 1911). For a useful critique see H.G.S. Aitken, *Taylorism at Watertown Arsenal*, Harvard University Press (Cambridge 1960).
12. F.J. Roethlisberger and W.J. Dickson, *Management and the Worker*, John Wiley and Sons (New York 1964).
13, *Ibid.*, p. 87.

14. *Ibid.*, pp. 58–9.
15. E.L. Trist and K.W. Bamforth, 'Some Social and Pyschological Consequences of the Longwall Method of Coal Getting', *Human Relations*, Vol 4, (1951), pp. 3–38.
16. *Job Reform in Sweden*, Swedish Employers' Confederation (Stockholm 1975), p. 67.
17. *Ibid.*, pp. 118–119; also J.P. Norstedt and S. Agurén, *The Saab-Scania Report*, Swedish Employers' Confederation, (Stockholm 1973).
18. W.H. Starbuck, *Organisational Growth and Development*, Penguin Books (Harmondsworth 1971).
19. W.G. Bennis, 'A Funny Thing Happened on the Way to the Future', p. 97, in J.M. Thomas and W.G. Bennis, *Management of Change and Conflict*, Penguin Books (Harmondsworth 1972), pp. 92–120.
20. Opinion Research Centre, *What About the Workers?*, Dragonfly Publications (London 1975).
21. G.K. Ingham, *Size of Industrial Organisation and Worker Behaviour*, Cambridge University Press (Cambridge 1970).
22. See L.R. Sayles and G. Strauss, *Human Behaviour in Organisations*, Prentice-Hall (Englewood Cliffs 1966), pp. 361–78.
23. Ingham, *op. cit.*, Chapter 8.
24. See, for example, *Classification of Occupations and Directory of Occupational Titles*, *Vols 1–3*, HMSO (London 1972).
25. W.H. Scott, J.A. Banks, A.H. Halsey, T. Lupton, *Technical Change and Industrial Relations*, (Liverpool 1956), Appendix A.
26. *Ibid.*, p. 264.
27. For a discussion of occupational identification see J.E. Hebden, 'Patterns of Work Identification', *Sociology of Work and Occupations*, Vol 2, (1975), pp. 107–32.
28. H.S. Becker and J.W. Carper, 'The Development of Identification with an Occupation', *American Journal of Sociology*, Vol 61, (1956), pp. 289–98.

6   Preparing for participation

Introduction

In this chapter, we shall be outlining a strategy for preparing for participation. In doing so, we have two sorts of organisation in mind. First, there is that which would not claim to be practising a participative style of management, where there are few manifestations of participative decision-making and where the question is being asked, possibly for the first time in any conscious way, 'what are we going to do about participation?' Second, there is the organisation which considers itself to practise participation to some degree, where there is at least some *prima facie* evidence of participative decision-making but where it is being increasingly felt that in the light of the trends in the industrial environment which we discussed in the last chapter and bearing in mind recent legislation and likely further legislation requiring more consultation and information disclosure, the time has come for a thoroughgoing review of the organisation's position on the matter.

But why bother doing anything at all? Why have a strategy for preparing for participation? Why not allow participation to develop in a 'natural' evolutionary manner? The view of the authors is that while it may have been possible fifteen, ten or even five years ago to ignore the issue of participation altogether or take a *laissez-faire* approach to it, nowadays the issue can no longer be ignored, nor is it good management to opt for a 'let's-take-it-as-it-comes' philosophy. The difference between now and fifteen years ago is that now, management is far less able to control the pace at which participation is developed. It is trends outside its control that are now setting the pace and which point to the need for managements to recognise these trends and respond to them in a proactive rather than a reactive way. In other words, the development of participation should be managed; it should not simply be allowed to happen.

Preparing for participation involves far more than grafting onto the company a set of new procedures and institutions. It involves making fundamental changes in the way that the company conducts its affairs. So it is no simple and smooth exercise with simple and smooth solutions. As we saw in Chapter 5, every company is unique because of the complex interplay of a range of structural variables such as size, markets, location, technology, organisation, industrial relations tradition and so on, which produce no two companies alike. This means that every company has to develop its own unique approach to participation. There are no blueprints. There are no off-the-peg solutions. What works well in company X is good for company X. That is all we can say about it – except that it could be at best irrelevant and at worst disastrous if applied elsewhere. While it makes good sense to learn from the experiences of participation gained by other companies, (and we shall be discussing subsequently some problems and pitfalls in developing participation), there is a world of difference between learning from the experience of other companies and borrowing from their practices. It is up to each company to carry out its own study aimed at producing a tailor-made approach suitable to its own needs. Nancy Taylor writes:

'Talk to any company, be it a great multinational or a family concern, which has already gone down this road and they have one thing in common – with hindsight they would have done it differently! Common threads are insufficient prior investigation and analysis, too little involvement of middle managers and front line supervisors, over-concern with either technical or with social aspects to the detriment of the other, failure to foresee the effect of changes in one department on other departments and groups and more especially the effect on their formal pattern of industrial relations. All stress the uniqueness of their own organisation and the importance of timing and training. In other words, initial depth or viability studies would have avoided unnecessary set-backs, time and money.'[1]

So how does one set about such a viability study? Let us consider how not to set about it. Firstly, a viability study should not be an all-management exercise. The decision to make a study is a management decision but for management exclusively to carry it out and then implement its results or findings is to make a nonsense of participation. For companies with a tradition of joint regulation by management and employee representatives, the very idea would be a non-starter. Something else to be avoided is an over-reliance on specialists whether from inside the company such as personnel or training specialists, or from outside such as consultants.

Pigors and Myers discuss this issue as it concerns relationships between personnel administration and line managers. They note that,

'the success of a personnel administrator in any organisation is measured by the extent to which he has helped every manager to become a good administrator of personnel'.[2]

The danger, they suggest, is that personnel specialists will cease to *help* line managers in their personnel management and will *do* the personnel management for them.[3]

Similarly in the development of participation, we do not suggest that one should avoid the use of specialist advisers but we would make the point that if participation is to be effective, all concerned in the process must feel they have ownership of it. When a specialist is employed, therefore, his role, should be to help and advise rather than to dominate or attempt to 'sell' particular approaches or packages. Broadly speaking there are three ways in which a specialist or specialists can carry out a role based on such help or advice.

First, a specialist can act as an information resource. This entails providing information about participation, alternative approaches to it, how they work in practice, their implications in terms of the possibilities and pitfalls which they may present. It entails helping people to understand and relate the experience of participation gained in other companies and countries to their own company context.

A second way in which a specialist might help is as a trainer. If preparing for participation is to do with making radical changes in the way of life of a company, the way in which decisions are made, who is involved and the information available to them, new skills and attitudes must be learnt. In particular, participation demands a high quality of teamwork and representative skills if it is to work effectively. It demands a management style that is in tune with its philosophy – for example by emphasising delegation, decision-making based on knowledge rather than position in the organisation, the importance of free expression of viewpoints and mutual support and collaboration – rather than a management style hostile to it. Preparing for participation can thus be thought of as a learning process, and a complex and difficult one at that. Where the trainer can help – and we are talking of a very high calibre of trainer – is in things like helping people to learn about participation through tackling real problems, developing their conceptual understanding of participation and the skills involved, preparing learning objectives and programmes and, not least, passing on his skills to others so that participation can become self-generating. We examine these skills more fully in Chapter 8.

Thirdly, a specialist can provide help as a catalyst or sounding board. This might involve activities such as advising on alternative lines to take at critical stages in preparing for participation and helping people to work out for themselves the relative advantages and disadvantages of each. It might involve at certain times playing a devil's advocate role or helping people to face up to inconsistencies between the standards that they have set for their own behaviour and the way in which they actually behave. Almost certainly it will involve giving people honest feedback on how they exercise their skills as team members or as representatives.

The selection of a specialist or specialists to help in preparing for participation – and, indeed, the decision as to whether to call on specialist help at all – needs very careful consideration. It should be remembered that the development of participation is a long-term process. Apart from any other roles, it is useful for an outsider to come into the organisation from time to time and help people stand back from the detail and make occasional course corrections. But whatever role they play it is important that such specialist roles are discussed at the outset and agreed. In OD terminology, a 'psychological contract' must be made. Moreover this discussion should involve all parties; it is essential in the development of participation to establish credibility from the outset. This agreement may need to be regularly reviewed jointly thereafter up to the point where the specialist is no longer needed.

Establishing a steering group

Having looked at some of the drawbacks inherent in carrying out a viability study as a purely management exercise or allowing specialists to dominate, let us now look at what the alternative approach might be. If the object of the exercise is to prepare the company for participation, then there is logic in doing this in a participative way – starting as you intend to go on. This can be accomplished through the use of a representative steering group (large dispersed companies may need several steering groups) to manage the preparatory stages of participation. Groups of this sort have basically three tasks. The first is to establish benchmarks or reference points for the development of participation in terms of defining where the company is now as far as participation is concerned (i.e. its prevailing philosophies and practices of participation), and where by contrast, it would like the company to be. The second task is to get action under way to develop participation within the company using the two benchmarks that it has established as a guide. And the third task is to monitor this action ensuring that it maintains both direction and momentum until the point when it becomes self-sustaining, thus making the steering group redundant. We shall return to these three tasks of the steering group in more detail later. Let us examine meanwhile the key features of a steering group.

Above all, it should be representative. It is vital that all parties which are able significantly to influence the organisation's effectiveness in terms of its survival, growth and profitability, participate. It is vital too that the steering group carries the authority to enable it to fulfil its second function of getting action under way to develop participation within the organisation. Thus a prerequisite of any steering group is that it reflects the power structure of the organisation. Its authority is reduced to the extent

that significant groupings feel that they are insufficiently
represented or not represented at all. For this reason, if for
no other, companies with established trade unions should
ensure trade union involvement on such a steering group.
To fail to do this at the outset could result in the
development of a dual system similar to the joint
consultation–collective bargaining division discussed in
Chapter 3 and with similarly weakening effects on the
participative institutions.

Secondly, membership of the steering group should be
limited to ten or twelve at the outside. Beyond twelve, it
becomes difficult if not impossible for each member to play
a full part. For some establishments, the large multi-union
factory for example, or a large hospital, the achievement of
setting up a steering group which is acknowledged as
representative and which is composed of a maximum of ten
to twelve members can be no mean feat. But it is worth
spending time and effort to meet these two criteria rather
than taking premature action which could prejudice the
steering group's subsequent effectiveness.

The third key feature of a steering group is that is
requires from its members an outlook of co-operation
rather than one of conflict. As we noted in Chapter 1, all
organisations will be characterised by elements of conflict
and elements of consensus. This expresses itself in a real
way on such a steering group which is not a negotiating
group although some of its members may play a
negotiating role in other contexts. The basic question to
which a steering group addresses itself, which could be
expressed as 'What sort of participation do we want to see
here and how are we going to get it?', demands creativity
and a full contribution of the abilities of each member.
These attributes are not likely to emerge where members
approach the steering group with a win-lose mentality.

A steering group can provide through its work an

excellent vehicle for its members to learn about participation. Because of its representative nature, it can be seen as a microcosm of the organisation, having to make decisions and find answers to problems by balancing a whole range of interests and making best use of the resources available. A trainer, skilled in group processes, can make a particularly useful contribution in the early stages of the work of a steering group and in the authors' experience, there is a good argument for a steering group to undergo a short period of training before it sets to work. This training should aim to broaden the steering group members' understanding of group processes (e.g. the relationship between group objectives and group structure and the uses of alternative types of decision-making) and representation. Perhaps the best way to learn *about* participation is by applying it in a real task. This is just what the steering group is doing as it sets about its business.

Additionally, the steering group, if it is to be successful, will demonstrate the advantages and problems involved in developing high levels of trust, goodwill and an understanding of other people's points of view.

A critical issue for the operations of the steering group is the appointment of a chairman. We would approach this matter in terms of what the chairmanship role involves in such groups. A distinction may be made between the leadership that the group requires in particular tasks and the basic 'housekeeping' needs of the group. These latter needs involve arranging meetings, formally liaising with outside specialist consultants, maintaining records and the like. The group will determine how big such a housekeeping role is to be. But the essential leadership role concerns the substantive tasks that the group is to perform. We believe that this should evolve where possible to meet the needs of the group in dealing with specific tasks. It could be wrong to assume that the individual looking after the housekeeping affairs of the group would automatically be the appropriate leader for each of the tasks with which the group must deal. Once again the steering group will be able to learn by doing. It will be able to implement the view that participation succeeds by permitting individual potential to be developed in the interests of the organisation's larger objectives.

Two other features of a steering group should be mentioned. The first is that it is not a permanent group. It is a temporary *ad hoc* group brought together with a specific job to do and when it is completed it should be disbanded. The appropriate time to disband a steering group will always be a matter of fine judgment The task of a steering group is to guide the company in developing relevant forms of participation capable of doing the job that they are intended to do and capable of self-regulation and self-improvement. The steering group has to judge when this task is sufficiently well on its way to achievement to enable it to bow out.

The last feature which we want to mention is concerned with communication between the steering group and the organisation at large. There is a danger with groups of any sort that they become the object of mistrust, misunderstanding and suspicion on the part of those outside. In theory this should not happen with groups composed of individuals charged with representing people outside the group; but in practice representatives for a variety of reasons fail to fulfil their role. We have already suggested that representational skills are an important part of the training of steering group members. We will suggest below that such skills are an important part of the training of all those who are involved in these aspects of participation. A steering group, charged with giving a lead on participation should put particular emphasis on maintaining a high quality of representation and on communications outside the group. It can only succeed in its job if it carries the organisation as a whole with it. It will not do this automatically; it has to make a conscious effort to do it.

We now return to the three tasks that a steering group has to do.

Establishing benchmarks

The first of the three steering group tasks, as we stated on page 165, is the establishment of benchmarks for the development of participation within the company. This involves the steering group in asking itself two questions: 'where do we stand *now* on participation and where would we *like to be*?' In other words, what progress has been achieved to date in extending participation in the company and what long-term goals should we set? The aim of the first question is to bring out the various problems and possibilities currently prevailing that will inevitably have an influence on any further developments in participation; the aim of the second is to establish clear directions to enable such developments to take place in a co-ordinated rather than a piecemeal and haphazard way. By so doing everyone can be agreed on what it is that the organisation is heading for.

The two questions should be tackled quite separately rather than simultaneously since in the authors' experience it is almost impossible for any group to focus adequately on one of the questions when half of its thoughts and attentions are focussed on the other. In tackling each of the two questions though, there are five major aspects of participation which a steering group should take into account in order to answer them comprehensively. These are:

1. Philosophy of participation
2. Participation in practice

3.   People and participation
4.   Participation and the internal environment of the
      organisation
5.   Participation and the external environment of the
      organisation

Let us look at each of these aspects.

Philosophy of participation By philosophy, we mean a set of
beliefs or values which serves as a guideline for practice and
in terms of which practice can be understood and
explained. In order fully to understand and make valid
judgments on the organisation's current participation
practices, the steering group should aim to identify the
philosophy or philosophies which they express. Are the
organisation's participative practices, for example, an
expression of a philosophy which sees employee
involvement in decision-making as intrinsically right and
proper? Industrial democracy, for example, may be seen as
an end in its own right. It is simply a value position which
requires no further justification. Alternatively, is
participation seen in the organisation as a means to an end?
Is it expected to produce more profitable firms, more
effective public utilities, improved services in hospitals and
social service departments? And what do organisations
mean by participation anyway? Is it to do with a limited
employee involvement in taking a limited number of
decisions or is it co-ordination on critical, strategic
decisions? How far are the beliefs that individuals express
about participation – e.g. 'I believe in an open door policy
as far as all my staff are concerned' or 'As a shop steward I
feel I have a responsibility to give an accurate
representation of what my members are saying' – borne
out in practice?
    These are some of the questions that were posed and
discussed at some length in Chapter 1. They need to be

asked and thought through by every organisation debating an extension of participation.

But besides looking at the prevailing philosophy (or philosophies) of participation within the organisation, the steering group should also ask itself what sort of philosophy it would *like* to see obtaining. This involves thinking about possible criteria by which participation practices within the organisation might in future be judged. Such criteria would be concerned for example with rights to consultation and information and mutual responsibilities to each other of management and employee representatives.

For some people, the very word 'philosophy' may seem to have only a remote connection with the issues of everyday industrial life. But participation, if it is anything, is to do with values and beliefs about the relationship between individuals and organisations. Unless a steering group can get to grips with participation at a philosophical level (i.e. 'Why are we doing it?', 'What do we want to achieve by it?') its contribution in terms of guiding the enterprise in the development of its practices of participation is bound to be diminished.

Participation in practice This aspect of participation concerns issues on which participation takes place, the extent to which it takes place and the machinery for handling it. Since the last war there has been a marked trend towards a widening of the scope of the issues on which participation in companies typically takes place. Similarly, the extent to which it takes place has widened as well so that nowadays issues which would have been considered as coming under the heading of managerial prerogatives have become subject to joint regulation of various degrees. Recent legislation such as the Employment Protection Act, the Industry Act and the Health and Safety at Work Act has accelerated this process. Machinery for handling participation differs widely of course from company to company, reflecting as we have seen factors such as size, industrial relations tradition, technology and philosophy. Participative machinery, furthermore, may be well-developed at one level but not so well-developed at others.

As regards this aspect of participation, a steering group should consider on the one hand the relevance of the organisation's current participative practices and how well they are working. On the other hand, it should consider what sort of participative practices it would like to see established in the organisation in line with its ideas on where the organisation should be heading as far as its philosophy of participation is concerned. It is important for the credibility of the whole programme that practice and philosophy should not be too far apart. For the same reasons it is important to develop an organisation-wide approach. Holes in the programme, either at particular levels or in particular departments will hinder the development of trust by casting doubt on the seriousness of management's intentions.

In the industrial situation, however, a company may be involved in operations in a variety of industries and thus be experiencing different environmental demands, as discussed in the last chapter, from situation to situation.

The example of the freight distribution company described on page 156 above illustrates the way in which modest credibility may be maintained while establishing nevertheless quite wide-ranging objectives.

People and participation Philosophies and practices of participation are mediated through people. The quality of participation in any company depends very much on the quality of personal relationships at all levels and on people's ability to contribute relevant skills. Machinery for handling participation, unlike any other machinery, will only do the job that it is designed to do if it is operated by sufficient people with the necessary levels of commitment as well as ability. Questions for a steering group to consider here could include who represents whom on what issues, and how much training and support do they get to do their job? And in the light of what the steering group would like to see obtaining in the company in its philosophy and practices of participation, what would be the implications in terms of skills and attitudes that would need to be developed by the people involved?

Training, of course is by no means a cost-free activity nor can it be carried out instantly. Designing programmes, obtaining good training materials and trainees takes time. Moreover the skills and commitments that are to be imported are not simple mechanical ones. The time taken for such training has implications for the implementation programme that the steering group will be working towards. The group will also need to face the 'bottleneck' problem. How many people need to be trained before the participative process is launched.? If too many people are trained ahead of time they can get frustrated and stale. If too few, there will not be enough to make the programme work.

Finally the steering group should consider the rotation of representatives in order that experience of involvement may be shared and greater amounts of talent brought to bear on the problems facing the organisation. If this is to be done, training will become a continuing activity for which provision will need to be made.

Participation and the internal environment In Chapter 5 we discussed at length the ways in which factors in the internal environment of organisation held implications for participation. Technology, size, occupational structure and the tradition of industrial relations combine uniquely in every organisation to produce a particular setting within which management is required to act.

An important activity for the steering group is to

establish the ways in which such variables affect their ability
to achieve participation in their own case and to seek a
policy to deal with this. Such policy may involve adjusting
their aspirations to meet their situation, or achieving some
adjustment in both. Solutions do not need to be as extreme
as those at Volvo or Saab-Scania. Their major programmes
of reconstruction, it should be remembered, have followed
many years of modest adjustment to organisation, to the
form of labour management relations and to the physical
environment. For the most part, Scandinavian forms of
direct participation have been achieved by incremental
changes within the framework of the internal environment.
They have thus, over time, brought about significant
extensions of participation.

A recognition and agreement about the parameters of
the situation in which they must operate is the first step
towards creative schemes for participation.

The internal environment, furthermore, should not be
seen in a purely negative way as restricting opportunities.
Each of the elements in the environment may be
approached as an opportunity for the development of
participation. Such an identification of the critical elements
in the social system of the organisation is an activity in
which outside consultants may be especially useful. Their
role, however, should not be to tell the steering group what
these elements are – much less what should be done about
them. Rather the consultant can help the group members
discover for themselves the significance of features of their
situation to which they have become inured over time.

Participation and the external environment Such consultants can
play a similar role for the steering group in recognising the
constraints of the external environment. Again, the
elements of the external environment may be interpreted
as providing opportunities which can be exploited for the
development of a more participative management style.

Unlike the elements of the internal environment, however, there is less that the group can do, to obtain a change in circumstances. While one may obtain either small or quite major changes in technology, reorganisation of management structure and, in time, a change in traditional industrial relations attitudes, elements of the external environment are less easily altered. Cultural patterns, product markets or national industrial relations issues are matters within which participation must exist or through which it might be made to thrive.

In Appendix I, a check-list of questions and points to consider is set out covering each of the five aspects of participation discussed above.

Getting action under way

Having now established benchmarks, the next task of a steering group is to initiate action to extend and improve participation within the company. In other words, having tackled the two questions of 'where are we now?' and 'where would we like to be?' the next question to be tackled is 'how are we going to get there?' The possible lines of action that a steering group might initiate at this stage in its work are infinite. They might include, for example, action ranging from getting training organised for representatives to setting up a new works council embracing both negotiating and consultative roles, from forming departmental productivity groups to launching company-level representative teams to devise (say) a new job evaluation scheme or grievance procedure.

This second task for the steering group may be more difficult than that described in the earlier sections of this chapter. Up to this point the steering group has been relatively private – essentially concerned with relationships between themselves as the members came to terms with their roles and sought to carry out the necessary studies and then discuss their implications. Some members may well have difficulty in these new styles of relationships – managers in the presence of employees and *vice versa*. The development of such teamwork roles is mentally demanding. It involves the participants in personal risks as they answer the question 'how far can I go?' in the new situation and the new relationships.

But these are private problems. Sooner or later the steering group must publicise its views. It must get itself committed to participation before fellow managers and work-mates.

Two things are now put to the test. Firstly the quality of the teamwork development that has taken place within the group during the completion of its first task. If the group has worked hard to build up levels of trust, open communications and understanding of each others' points of view and taken risks, the more likely it is that the necessary degree of commitment will be there to sustain whatever action the group initiates. On the other hand, commitment to action is bound to be lacking if the work of the steering group has been characterised by low levels of trust and involvement and mutual recriminations throughout.

The second thing to be put to the test is the quality of representation that has gone on so far to link the work of the steering group to the people outside it. As we pointed out above it is very easy for any group to become introverted and take on a life of its own and these are pitfalls to be avoided at all costs by a steering group. Thorough consultation throughout by the members of the steering group of those whom they are representing helps to ensure that the group's contribution to the development of participation in the company meets the twin criteria of relevance and acceptability.

There are a number of principles worth observing by a steering group in carrying out its second task of initiating action. The first of these is to build on success. Where existing participation practices work effectively and acceptably, then the logic is for these to be retained and developed even if current management fads and fashions might suggest otherwise.

A large firm making electrical components illustrates the point. A working party in the company deliberated for some time and finally announced a long-term plan with a blaze of publicity. Ten year objectives were announced and shorter three and five year goals were stated as a means of achieving these. Although the plan had the blessing of top management, it frightened the middle management layer which feared for their position and took action to resist the plan. It aroused cynicism at the shop-floor where the plan was regarded as a management ploy.

The scheme failed to meet its intermediate targets and the cynicism was reinforced. Among the members of the working party, disillusionment was rife and members began to resign. When the project was abandoned, the firm did not return to zero, but to a position which was a considerable deterioration on its starting point.

By starting in a small way with problems that are capable of some short-term success, but which people recognise as real, confidence can be established in the concept. By building on success, progress can be quickly made which will engender support for more difficult targets.

This is not to suggest that long-term objectives should be ignored. It is important that a vision exists and institutional changes should be put in hand. But more immediately, the steering group should work to getting attitudes right, to establishing the atmosphere receptive to the bigger scheme.

Second, where new participative practices are to be initiated, these should be left as simple as possible and their functions described in terms which are in everyday use in the company. What a steering group should avoid is the launching of ambitious new participation programmes involving elaborate documentation and publicity. An organisation can only cope with a limited amount of change at any one time. The pace at which new participative practices are developed must take account of this fact.

Third, any new participative practices should focus on real issues to which those involved can contribute knowledgeably and which they have the capability to influence. This is one way in which the 'constraints' of the internal environment can begin to be seen as opportunities for the development of participation. If participation comes to be seen as something separate from, and only marginally related to, what happens at work, people will lose interest and become cynical about it. This, as we have seen, has been the fate suffered by joint consultation in many companies. Furthermore, there is little point in having people taking part in working parties, committees or meetings where they lack the know-how to contribute usefully or where, if they have a contribution to make, the chances of this having a bearing on the outcome of the deliberations are slight.

Long-term plans may well be ambitious. The steering group may well decide that the kind of total, integrated system of participation that we have advocated here should be adopted as a goal. But the group should be wary of publicising such ultimate objectives at the outset. There may be circumstances where this could be done and the steering group must decide this. But there is a strong case for starting with modest objectives which are capable of demonstrating early success.

Monitoring the action

The third task of a steering group is to monitor the development of participation within the company. By 'monitoring' we mean a role which is to do with helping, guiding and stimulating rather than a role which is inspectorial and regulatory, to do with keeping things tidy and uniform. Any steering group runs the risk of being seen by those outside as the 'owners' of participation, the fountain-head, the source of knowledge. In order to overcome this problem, the steering group must take pains to ensure that people have the chance to shape and influence participative activities in which they are involved, learning from experience, making improvements and adjusting to new situations. So monitoring in this context is far removed from the imposition of rules, constitutions and procedures to check and regulate what goes on in practice. Rather, the aim of a steering group should be as a catalyst to help those involved in participative activities to develop their own monitoring procedures. It can do this by laying on appropriate training – and not necessarily through specialist trainers. A number of organisations have successfully used steering group members as trainers, passing on the skills that they have learnt through their membership of the steering group. Besides this, a steering group can assist the development of participation in other ways: by serving as a channel for the flow of information and ideas on participation and by diffusing throughout the company lessons learnt as people broaden their experience of participation.

As soon as a sense of ownership of participation begins to take hold on the part of people at large within the company, the steering group should think of winding itself up. Once people can manage participation for themselves, there is no need for a steering group to continue to manage it for them.

References

1. N. Taylor, 'Time to Prepare for Participation', *Personnel Management*, Vol 8, (August 1976), p. 3.

2. P. Pigors and C.A. Myers, *Personnel Administration*, McGraw-Hill (London 1961), p. 31.
3. The problem of providing 'help' to line managers is also discussed in D. McGregor, *The Human Side of Enterprise*, McGraw-Hill (New York 1960), Chapters 11 and 12.

7 Problems in developing participation

Introduction

If participation were simply a matter of grafting new institutions and procedures on to a company without fundamentally changing it, its introduction would be a relatively simple matter. But as we have stated previously, it involves much more than that; it is to do with changing the way of life of a company, the way in which decisions are taken, the way in which work gets done, the way in which people treat each other. It demands a questioning of existing attitudes and the development of new ones. It requires people to develop new skills which hitherto they may not have needed. Perhaps above all it presents a high level of uncertainty which brings with it fear and apprehension. It is small wonder that, when the subject of participation is discussed, feelings and emotions figure strongly.

In this chapter we shall be discussing what we see as typical pitfalls and problems that arise when companies decide to move along the participation road and we shall attempt to point out some lessons. But it is perhaps worth re-stating that there are no blueprints or royal roads to participation. We believe that the experience of companies that have already made some progress in developing participation can provide useful learning for others contemplating a move in this direction. There is no substitute, however, for learning from one's own experience and each company must work out its own approach to participation in the light of its own unique circumstances.

Participation and the manager

In the authors' experience, it is rare for managers outside those companies which have had successful experiences of participation to express any enthusiasm for an extension of participation in their own companies. A myriad of drawbacks and reasons why it will not work in *our* company are adduced; the potential disadvantages seem only too plain and any likely advantages are only dimly perceived or not perceived at all. But there are good reasons why managers typically take this outlook. For some, participation is seen as a threat to 'managerial prerogatives', an infringement of management's 'right to manage'. For others, it is nothing short of a political threat, a left-wing and trade union inspired movement aimed at a take-over of industry by the unions.

But even for the manager who finds little use or relevance in today's world in the concept of managerial prerogatives, and who can see beyond the newspaper reports and television debates and recognise that people's aspirations towards more participation cannot be simply explained away as politically motivated, the concept of participation does pose some misgivings.

For a start, the manager may feel more exposed when decisions that he has been used to making on his own become subject to consultation and even to criticism from sources he has hitherto ignored. And even though decisions through consultation may be better decisions, at least where acceptability on the part of those affected is the main criterion, consultation does tend to slow down decision-making. For the manager who needs to know everything that goes on in his factory or department, who feels that he must be in control and who puts a high premium on order, participation holds some deep psychological drawbacks because it means letting go of the reins, allowing people to make more decisions for themselves and giving them more discretion. If one's life and work experience have led to the conclusion that people on the whole need to be directed and that they want to be managed and have decisions made for them, the philosophy which says that people can take on far more challenge and responsibility than their work normally allows simply flies in the face of that experience. Participation schemes which seek to build up the discretionary element in people's jobs cannot get very far unless management attitudes are in sympathy.

At a plastics factory in the Midlands, the Production Manager and Quality Control Manager, concerned over unacceptably high levels of scrap produced in the Moulding Department, devised proposals for the moulders themselves to carry out the routine quality control checks hitherto carried out by quality control staff. The idea was that the moulders should in effect take responsibility for the quality of their own output rather than quality control staff whose jobs would in future focus on the non-routine aspects of quality control.

The Production Manager and the Quality Control Manager took considerable pains to discuss their ideas with the moulders themselves, the quality control staff and trade union representatives and got a favourable response. The Factory Manager however saw little merit in the proposals, taking the view that to allow moulders to carry out routine quality checks themselves would only aggravate the problem of scrap. He further insisted that he should have the final say, where customers were calling for delivery urgently and there was some doubt about the product meeting specification, as to whether the product should go or not. Nevertheless, the Production and Quality Control managers persuaded him at least to give their proposals a trial. A training programme was mounted for the moulders and the proposals implemented.

Results at first were dramatic with scrap levels falling by up to seventy-five per cent and the moulders reporting a marked increase in job satisfaction. However, the Factory Manager's misgivings concerning the moulders' taking on what was previously a Quality Control Department responsibility did not diminish and during a period when the Company was under pressure to meet a heavy customer demand, he took it upon himself a number of times to countermand moulders' decisions to reject certain batches. Gradually, the moulders began to lose interest in their new quality control role, taking the view that there was little point in being trained to make, and being asked to make, decisions which might then be reversed from above. Further improvements projected in output and scrap levels did not materialise within the Moulding Department and the Production and Quality Control Managers decided to abandon plans to extend the scheme to other departments.

This example illustrates well the point that has been emphasised repeatedly in this book; participation is an organisation-wide activity and as such cannot be confined to particular departments or to particular levels. If one does this, there is the need for an interface between the participative and the traditional systems. This will not only be a point of conflict and strain but also, as in the plastics factory described above, a source of ultimate breakdown of the system.

A dramatic example of the problem of interface is provided by Strauss in his description of an extension of participation in the paint shop of a toy factory.[1] The very success of this scheme brought about its downfall as rises in production began to have their effect on adjacent departments. Increased production in the department also had its effect on pay differentials throughout the company. Strauss notes, 'the changes made in the paint room implied an overall managerial attitude and philosophy that were not in fact present. This being the case, there was no conceptual or philosophic resource for dealing with the eventual implications of what had been done in the paint room.'[2]

Strauss concludes,

'the factory is a social system, made up of mutually dependent parts. A drastic change in one part of the system – even a change that is highly successful within that part – may give rise to conflict reactions from other parts of the system. It may then be dangerous for management to try a new approach in one small part of the system unless it is prepared to extend this approach to the whole organisation.'[3]

In seeking to involve each level of management in the participation programme, a particular source of difficulty has been found at the middle level. Involving workers in decision-making above the supervisory level has obvious implications for the supervisor who may be the last person to know of changes that will affect him. Extending jobs below his level runs the risk of reducing the supervisor's job still further and raising anxiety and unhelpful defensive reactions.

But this need not inevitably be the case. A key feature of the experience of ICI at Gloucester was the extent to which middle management and supervision were involved throughout the change programme.[4] Supervisors in fact played an important role in leading shop-floor discussions to explain management's ideas and to explore ways in which workers could improve working methods both to increase efficiency and job satisfaction. The supervisors had undertaken a year's training, most of it on the job before being appointed supervisors as well as receiving special training in group discussion leadership. All this is in sharp contrast to what the authors have found happening so frequently in industry where change programmes are initiated by top management and, far from being involved in their design and implementation, the supervisor claims that he is the last to learn about them.

The ICI decision to involve their supervisors in the way that they did was, in effect, to see the supervisors as an opportunity rather than a problem. Thus instead of being seen as a barrier or obstacle between senior management and the shop-floor, somehow to be by-passed in order that communication between the top and the bottom of the pyramid may be established, the supervisors were used as a communications link. In using the supervisors in this way, the senior management was doing nothing more than recognising the reality of the plant's organisation structure: that a major change programme could not be brought about successfully without carefully considering the implications for all levels; that middle management and supervision could play a key role – given training and senior management backing.

The relationship between the quality of middle management and supervision, and the success or otherwise of participation schemes, is illustrated by the contrasting experience of two medium-sized textile firms in the North of England, the first a family-owned concern and the second a subsidiary of a large corporation but enjoying considerable autonomy. At about the same time both firms introduced similar participation schemes. In each case there was a profit-sharing element but the main feature of the two schemes involved the setting up of works councils supported at departmental level by representative committees chaired by the departmental manager. The idea was that such managers should, as far as possible, resolve issues coming up at their committee meetings themselves or with colleagues heading other departments, and that items to be handled by the works councils should have a company-wide relevance.

In the first company, the family concern, almost all of the managers and supervisors had come up from the shop-floor. They had spent all their working lives in the company and had had little or no management training to supplement what they had picked up through experience. The owner and chief executive enjoyed high prestige and had successfully guided the company through some difficult times. The managers and supervisors however acted very much as assistants to the chief executive rather than executives in their own right. They were used to being able to rely on him to take difficult decisions for them and to pronounce on issues of an inter-departmental nature.

The departmental committees set up under the participation scheme were a failure almost from the start. Matters, often trivial, which had no implications beyond their own departments would be constantly referred to the chief executive by managers and supervisors. Gradually, employees became cynical and disillusioned with the departmental committees when it became apparent that they were ineffective. Eventually, the committees simply fizzled out.

In the second company, the subsidiary of the large corporation, the general manager played quite a different role *vis-à-vis* his subordinate managers. His policy was to give his managers as much responsibility as they could handle and he placed great emphasis on simple but effective management controls and information procedures. His management philosophy was very much one of management by exception. Long before the participation scheme was introduced, a comprehensive management development programme had been established including agreed target-setting and performance review on a regular basis. A high proportion of the managers held qualifications and had experience of working in other firms.

By contrast to the first firm, the departmental committees worked well. Both managers and shop-floor workers saw them as a useful forum for discussing and resolving issues of common concern. The general manager took the view, after only one year of operation, that the new participation scheme had had a direct influence to the good on morale and communications and had contributed towards an improved profit position and, in turn, to employee earnings.

The main difference between the management teams in these two firms was that in the first, managers were in effect assistants to and therefore dependent on the chief executive. In the second, they were expected to manage. Their different backgrounds and training undoubtedly had a major bearing on the contrasting experience of the two firms. In the second firm, managers were clear as to their roles and confident in their technical know-how and managerial skills. This was by no means the case in the first firm where managers saw the participation scheme as a threat to them. They were correct in this perception because the scheme made demands on them with which they were not equipped to cope.

In fact, the participation of workers in the running of their companies, far from diminishing the role of the manager, puts extra burdens on it. Where companies have a strong paternalistic philosophy and managers are little more than messengers or mouthpieces for the boss, a concentrated and long-term effort should be made to develop a strong and self-confident management team before any participation scheme is introduced. And by 'long-term' we are talking about years not months. Senior managements frequently under-estimate the time needed to effect programmes aimed at changing or modifying a company's management style and philosophy and further under-estimate the degree of involvement needed on their part to make such programmes a success.

A firm of 600 employees, until recently a family business but now belonging to a large international company, launched a programme aimed at involving supervisors more extensively in management decision-making and to develop the supervisors as a team. Four groups were formed each consisting of supervisors from different departments. The groups were scheduled to meet for one afternoon a week and were asked to tackle and produce recommendations on four issues – operator recruitment and training, plant layout, machine servicing and paperwork flow. Each of these issues transcended departmental boundaries. On each of them too there was a widely held feeling in the company that improvement was needed. Senior management believed that the supervisors together could contribute substantially to securing these improvements.

In contrast to senior management's expectations of the four groups, little emerged from them. The meetings became shorter and less frequent. Supervisors began to produce all sorts of reasons to excuse their non-attendance. It became obvious however that many doubted the value of the meetings and complained that senior management did not take part and would not take any notice of whatever came out of the meetings anyway. Some of the supervisors found the experience of the meetings disorientating and unhelpful.

A number of lessons were learnt by senior management from what had happened in the four groups. They realised that it was asking too much of supervisors used only to handling largely routine matters within their own departments to enter into group problem solving activities (in which problems were complex and long-term) and come up with results. The groups called, in effect, for a number of skills which the supervisors lacked – assembling, analysing and interpreting data and information located in different parts of the company, pooling and using appropriate expertise, skills of creative thinking and interpersonal skills. The conclusion that senior management reached was that it should not write off the experience altogether but that managers also should be involved in further supervisor project group activities and that the supervisors should be given help and training in teamwork skills.

The experience of F. Olsen Ltd at its Millwall Terminal in the late 1960s illustrated very well not only the difficulties that can be encountered in helping supervisors adjust to a more participative climate of decision-making but also a strategy for coping with them.[5] In 1967, Olsen's introduced a unit loading system at its new berth at Millwall which involved doing away with the traditional system of slinging loose cargo through deck hatches. The new system demanded far more flexible working methods and was implemented only after lengthy negotiations with the trade unions. Management expected that the new system would have its teething troubles as far as the dockers were concerned but this was not the case; it was the supervisors who were finding it difficult to adapt to the new situation. They were reluctant to change to suit the new methods of work and it was apparent that they did not see themselves as part of management at all. Management was considering running courses for the supervisors but eventually decided on a different approach altogether after consulting with a training specialist from the National Ports Council.

The approach adopted by Olsen's placed the emphasis on helping the supervisory team focus on ways of improving their handling of issues of immediate concern to them using their own experience as a vehicle for learning. The trainer helped as a catalyst at the team meetings providing ideas and suggestions on the way in which the supervisors worked together and to enable them to get the most from their joint experience. He also acted as a go-between, relaying information to management on matters which had the consent of the supervisors. Eventually, senior management was invited to take part in the meetings which came to be held weekly during a lunch-time break. The meetings between the supervisors and senior management were at first difficult and strained but after four months, the beginnings of a joint policy on methods of work at the Terminal began to emerge.

The Olsen experience conveys a wealth of lessons about participation well beyond the implications just for managers and supervisors. It is also an interesting study in the effects of technological change. As far as the supervisors were concerned, the approach used, with its key elements of using real experience as a vehicle for learning, employing an outside catalyst and the involvement of senior management, paid off in terms of building up the confidence of the supervisors, helping them to feel part of the management team and enabling them to cope with a situation demanding a much more participative style of management.

The development of self-supervision at shop-floor level whereby workers take a greater responsibility for such things as the arrangement of daily rosters and machine manning does raise the question of whether extensions of participation at this level require fewer supervisors and fewer levels of supervision. Alternatively, in qualitative terms, does the enrichment of some jobs lead to the impoverishment of others?

The development of participation is but the latest of a succession of changes that have all tended to reduce the power and status of the supervisor. These trends were pointed out in 1945 by Roethlisberger in his classic article for the *Harvard Business Review*, 'The Foreman: Master and Victim of Double Talk'.[6] The same theme has been developed periodically ever since – the most recent being a report on the 'front-line manager' by the British Institute of

Management.[7] The growth of specialists in a variety of areas, the growth of shop-floor power and of labour legislation, are but some of the trends bringing about a contraction of the supervisor's position. An indicator of his decline is the extent to which he, the man in the middle, is by-passed by alternative communication systems. The danger that exists is that participation will cause this poor situation to deteriorate further.

But this need not be so. Scott noted in 1952 that,

> 'the success of formal consultation with employee representatives must depend on the attainment of more effective consultation within the ranks of management. Only if matters to be raised at formal meetings are previously discussed within the management group can the 'short-circuiting' of intermediate and lower management, and the consequent development of negative attitudes on their part, be avoided.'[8]

For an aware and prepared management, participation is an opportunity to reverse this gradual reduction of the supervisor's role. It may be true that a reduction in the technical aspects of his role is inevitable as a result of new production technology, computerised systems of planning, for example, or of cost control. But if, as a result, opportunities for a bigger role in personnel management are provided, then the development of participation can provide the means by which this will be accomplished.

It remains to be seen how far such radical experiences of job re-design as that already referred to by Volvo at Kalmar succeed in resolving, not only assembly line problems, but also these problems of middle management. Examples do exist, however, of participative schemes which have sought greater levels of middle management and supervisory involvement.

The cases of Olsen and ICI Gloucester referred to above illustrate the point. Here the roles that the supervisors had previously played were modified in line with the new circumstances. There was much less emphasis on the traditional monitoring functions and more on planning, training and joint problem solving. But supervisors emerged at the end of the change programmes with more confidence in themselves and feeling much more a part of the management team. It should be noted however that the senior managements in both companies took deliberate steps to help the supervisors with the changes demanded of them as a consequence of the extension of shop-floor participation. At the ICI Gloucester plant, senior management went further by actually involving the supervisors in introducing the change programme. There is an important lesson here. Supervisors, far from being unfortunate but inevitable casualties of shop-floor participation programmes, can make a contribution to their success. For this to happen, however, does demand that senior management recognise that the role of the supervisor must change and equally important, that supervisors need their help and backing in order to cope with this change.

This touches the very heart of the participation issue. It is to do with the relationships between people at all levels. Argyris has noted that the view that workers have of their supervisors is largely coloured by the relationships that supervisors enjoy with *their* supervisors.[9] The organisation is in these terms an indivisible whole.

The issue of whether participation leads to a reduction in the levels of supervision needs to be treated in a much wider sense. It is supervisors who tend to feel most threatened by the extension of shop floor participation, but all managers are supervisors in the sense of controlling subordinates' performance. The issue, therefore, should not be confined to the effects participation has on supervisory roles and levels of supervision, but extended to the total organisational implications of participation. It may be, as Thomason points out, that we need to revise our entire ways of thinking about organisations for participation to become an organisational fact of life. He postulates two alternatives:

> 'the first is that the middle will be thinned in terms of personnel, and the trend towards the development of administrative 'fact', which has been a feature of the past fifty years, may be reversed in the process. The more sensible alternative, consistent with a more systematic approach to the whole question of management, focuses upon a re-thinking of the administrative decision-structure of organisations. We have become used to thinking of organisational design in terms of bureaucracy and we therefore fail to appreciate that the peculiar conditions which sustained bureaucracy from about the 1880s onwards may no longer be with us to support anything.'[10]

We would accept this latter alternative. It reflects the kind of statement by Bennis to which we referred in Chapter 5. It is in line with pressures discussed there which are coming from other directions. Increasing technical and market change and a general rise in the levels of uncertainty experienced by managers mean that bureaucratic organisations become increasingly difficult to design and manage. The precise allocation of rights and duties and the creation of a hierarchy to co-ordinate these is out of line with the demands of such a changing environment. The need is rather increasingly for a larger commitment to the broader organisation than the individual department and for the development of relationships – including lateral relationships – which facilitate and enhance such a commitment. Participation is more readily achieved by organisations which are on this road. But the ultimate development of participation will involve all organisations in some such adaptation of conventional forms and structures.

Participation and the employee representative

Participation raises important issues for the role of the employee representative as regards his relationship with management, his relationship with the people whom he represents and his relationship with the trade union and its full-time officials. In each of these three relationships there exist throughout industry, and indeed society generally, traditional expectations of how the employee representative should act. But as we shall describe below, participation makes demands of the employee representative that challenge these expectations fundamentally.

Taking the role of the employee representative *vis-à-vis* management first, the dilemma, put crudely is how far his role is to oppose management and how far to collaborate with it. The view traditionally held by many trade unionists is that opposition and collaboration are irreconcilable and that the job of trade unions is opposition. Take for instance what the EETPU had to say on this question in its evidence to the Bullock Committee:

'First, there is the institutional impossibility of separating the boardroom consultation from the potential negotiating implications behind the issues under discussion. Second, there is the irreconcilable split loyalties of the worker directors themselves. They will find it immensely difficult to separate their boardroom responsibilities dictated by business priorities from their representative functions derived from their relationship with the work force. The pursuit of trade union objectives will not then be helped by the disunity created in such an atmosphere. And this ignores the crude disagreements that must occur on occasion with worker directors, in possession of all the information, being a party to a decision or a policy that is opposed by the collective bargainers. Far better in the interests of those affected by a managerial decision that the responsibility for that decision is firmly laid at the management's door; then the collective bargaining machinery can oppose and moderate the impact of the decision when necessary.' [11]

Daniel and McIntosh refer to this dilemma where employee representatives have been invited by management to take part in planning organisational change programmes:

'Trade unionists have been reluctant to become involved in the drawing up of plans for change, the definition of criteria for job evaluation or the joint evaluation of jobs. They have feared that they would become too committed to the changes or the decisions in advance and would be less able to defend and promote their members' interests subsequently. They would have weakened their case for demanding the highest price for change, or they would be in a weaker position to pursue members' grievances about their job evaluation if they or their colleagues had been involved in the process.' [12]

But if employee representatives and trade unions see the representative role in terms of an opposition to management, it must be said that this is how many managers see it as well. A common theme running through company submissions to the Bullock Committee was the view that the proper role of trade unions was to safeguard their members' interests – but not to become involved in management. As one company stated in its evidence:

> 'It has been our experience that Trade Unions have rightly maintained that their prime responsibility was to protect the interests of their members. They have avoided any possible involvement in the management of the Company, even to the extent that they considered any discipline of their members in regard to safety matters, e.g. the wearing of safety helmets, was a management responsibility and the Unions reserved their rights to defend a member thus disciplined.
>
> 'Our considered opinion is that the Unions serve their members best by not accepting management responsibilities and that any representation by them on the Boards of Directors would place their delegates in an inviduous position involving conflict of loyalties.'

Whenever two parties see their relationship as being on opposite sides of the fence, in terms of an 'I win, you lose' game, attitudes, expectations and behaviour patterns which reflect this basic stance became reinforced as the relationship develops. Moreover, the two parties develop increasing levels of skill appropriate to this stance – overstating one's case, covert objectives, hidden agendas, delaying tactics, threatening postures, demanding (and expecting to give) *quid pro quo*.

But as Walton and McKersie point out, bargaining situations in which the gain of one party represents the loss of the other party are infrequent.[13] There is usually *some* gain to both parties in achieving an agreement. It is true that a distributive kind of conflict will predominate in some negotiations. But in other situations, both parties can achieve significant pay-off from the negotiations. The authors give a number of examples of this situation.

The negotiation behaviour is quite different from that in the win-win situation. The problem facing the shop-steward as a representative in the participative procedures is that of combining the two styles. In the win-lose situation, both sides are resolving an issue to the dominant advantage of one side or another. In the win-win situation, problem solving will work to the advantage of both parties. It is in everybody's interests to obtain the best solution to the problem. This will be done by open behaviour, cards-on-the-table, high trust relationships. But can representatives combine these two kinds of behaviour? Can a representative's open behaviour be reconciled with bluff and deliberate exaggeration?

We suggest there is no choice other than to try. We have already discussed the alternative which is to institutionalise in separate organisational forms the predominantly win-lose and predominantly win-win situation. The effect has been for the conflict oriented institutions to drive out the consensus focussed body. This, we suggested earlier, was one explanation for the decline of joint consultation.

But for the participation to succeed some means of organising for consensus and for conflict is required. The alternative to separate arrangements must be a combined system. We should recognise the pressures that this imposes on the individual representatives when we are asking them as individuals to bear the strains that the duality of conflict and consensus impose.

Viewed in these terms, the employee representative can be seen to deserve, not just consideration but considerable time and training to adapt to the pressures of this role. That this can be done can be seen from the evidence of successful schemes. It requires, not just a personal development programme for individual representatives but the development of the network of relationships in which he or she is involved.

The typical self-image of the employee representative as

being almost an institutionalised opposition to management is reinforced by the way in which the people whom he represents see his role. Thus the union, or the employee representative as the union's visible presence in the company, is seen as an insurance or council for the defence to provide help and support in the case of any dispute with the management or in the case of injury arising at work. Furthermore, as Goldthorpe found in his sample, many workers have little interest in their trade unions other than as a means of protecting and advancing their material rewards from work.[14] What happens therefore is that the employee representative is almost strait-jacketed by the expectations of both management and workers into taking a narrow role confined to negotiating with management and protecting workers interest on pay, conditions of employment and generally those matters which Wellens includes in his term 'negative participation'. Moreover, trade unions at national level tend to see the employee representative in this restricted way. The evidence by the EETPU to the Bullock Committee from which we quoted above typifies the viewpoint of the majority of the trade unions which submitted evidence.

The consequence of this limited role accorded to the employee representative has been to put brakes on the development of employee involvement in problem solving activities that demand a 'you win, we all win' outlook, where teamwork, creativity and high levels of trust are required. And if management has been reluctant to extend participation in this direction, then it can equally be said that trade unionists have frowned on it as well. This is a pity because it seems to ignore the fact that while workers may see their own interests and those of management as being diametrically opposed in certain respects, and hence the need for collective protection, there also exist wide areas at work where employees perceive themselves and management as sharing common interests. As we stated in

Chapter 1, to see the management-worker relationship from a purely conflict standpoint is to forget that conflict and consensus can in fact coexist and do. If conflict is endemic, so too is consensus. When the conflict aspect is emphasised at the expense of the consensus aspect, the result is that the potential contribution that employees can make to the enhancement of both efficiency and their own job satisfaction is lost. So too is the opportunity for managers and workers to develop a mutual climate of trust and goodwill out of the experience of tackling common interest issues jointly focussing on and building on what they agree about rather than what they disagree about.

There is evidence, however, to support the view that employee representatives are, willy-nilly, playing an integrative win-win game as well as a distributive win-lose one. The Government Social Survey carried out in 1968 for Donovan concluded that, in general, shop-stewards tended to help labour relations rather than the opposite.[15] In response to the question of to what extent the shop-stewards helped management to solve its problems and run the firm more efficiently, sixty-eight per cent said 'quite a lot' and only six per cent thought that they were giving no help to management at all. Furthermore, the survey showed that the greater the extent of joint regulation, the more likely were shop-stewards to see themselves as a help to management.

When one considers that this positive aspect of the representative's role has hardly been developed at all in terms of training and preparation, one can face the prospect of properly developed and planned systems of participation with some confidence. One can look to the reasonable levels of success achieved at ICI, Olsen, Baxi[16] or Bristol Channel Ship Repairers and others where employee representatives have taken part in successful joint problem solving activities with members of management covering areas such as work organisation and methods, job evaluation, manning arrangements and job training, and have done it on a win-win rather than a win-lose basis. But where activities of this type have happened and have been perceived as successful by both parties, a number of important conditions have applied. Perhaps most important of these is that senior management has taken the initiative of inviting employees and their representatives to make a contribution on issues which hitherto they would have seen as coming within management's responsibility to determine and management's alone. Senior management has thus taken the view that if its objectives are to secure the consent and commitment of the work force to a greater degree in the running of the enterprise and to tap the latent abilities of its employees to the full, then managerial philosophies based on the concept of prerogatives and the right of management to manage do not offer any constructive help but rather a blind alley. It has similarly recognised the value of bringing into the decision-making process from the outset, when changes are being contemplated, those who are likely to be affected and those who can contribute relevant know-how and experience. This is in contrast to management making the decisions unilaterally and then presenting them as a *fait accompli* or selling them to the work-force.

At a factory employing some 750 people belonging to a large public company, it was decided to set up a project team to examine how the overall performance of one of the manufacturing departments could be improved.[17] The team consisted of various managers and specialists and had allocated to it two members of the company's central organisational development staff. The inclusion of shop-floor representatives was suggested at the start but none of the managers was enthusiastic about the idea and some were strongly opposed, arguing that the presence of shop-floor representatives would be inhibiting. Great care was taken to communicate the objectives of the project team throughout the factory. Interviews were carried out with operatives in the department on which the project was based and communication maintained throughout the project not only with the shop-steward of the department but with the union branch secretary as well. It had been agreed with them that no changes would be made arising from the project without the consent of the union and the men. When the project team reached the stage of being able to put proposals forward, a joint meeting was arranged of the project team, project department work-force and union officials. Although management had seen this as the first of several explanatory discussions, the meeting quickly developed into a classical negotiation meeting. The branch secretary was the spokesman and virtually the sole speaker from the shop-floor and this resulted in the Production Director responding in a similar way on the management 'side'. Discussion centred on the proposals did not occur. Instead it centred on the costings of the proposals and the likely rewards for the operatives.

After the meeting, the project team reconsidered its strategy *vis-à-vis* the operatives and union officials, realising that their own understanding of the proposals was based on months of analysis and consideration, a process which had not been shared with the shop-floor. To verify this, the project team over a period of many weeks carried out a series of discussions on the proposals with the shop-floor. The employees became quite enthusiastic about the new ideas and contributed many improvements. Eventually, the proposals were agreed and a programme of implementation finalised. The shop-steward did not take part in all of these discussions and the branch secretary opted to be uninvolved relying on the shop-steward to keep him in touch.

When the time came for the management and the union to negotiate the sharing of the rewards, it was recognised that for employees in the project department to receive their due share would upset differentials with the rest of the factory and thus be opposed. The project department operatives, realising that they would have to put their case to the branch for the proposals to go through, turned out in force to the branch meeting and gained agreement in principle to the negotiations of a bonus independent of the main production area. At the formal negotiations which followed between management and the union, much of the need for bargaining had been removed by the influence exerted by the shop-floor earlier on in gaining the changes they wanted. There was high consensus on what the shape of the pay system should be. The negotiations were much shorter than usual and the proposals accepted with only minor alterations.

This case presents an illuminating contrast between the attitude of the shop-floor and its representatives to the project team proposals before they were involved in the activities of the team and after, when the team had reviewed its strategy and then took deliberate steps to bring the shop-floor into its discussions. Merely observing the rules of good communication by ensuring that everyone in the factory, not least of all the project department employees, were kept fully in the picture, did not prevent the first meeting between the project team and the shop-floor and its representatives from becoming a stereotyped bargaining meeting. But once the shop-floor did get involved, it played a positive rather than a negative role, it was prepared to argue a case for the proposals at a branch meeting and the formal negotiating meeting at the end was much shorter and took on a much different flavour from the normal hard bargaining pursued by both sides on such occasions. It is interesting to note that at the end of the project, management, the shop-floor and the employee representatives all agreed that a similar project should be initiated in a second department and furthermore that it should be run from the outset by a *joint* project team consisting of representatives of management, employee representatives and the employees concerned.

If the change of strategy on the part of the managers and specialists composing the project team after the first joint meeting with the men and their representatives indicated a radical shift in their attitudes, an equally radical shift in attitudes was brought about on the part of the shop steward and the men as a result of their subsequent involvement with the project team members, when they were able to modify and improve their original proposals. The benefits gained by both sides ultimately were gained as the result of the initiatives made by the project team being reciprocated by the shop-steward and the men. This demanded of the shop-steward in particular a very different role from the one he was used to. Commenting on this aspect of the exercise Lovelady states:

'The shop-steward was being asked to move from the role of 'defender-advocate' and 'reactor' to management initiative into one of co-planner with inputs to make alongside other union members. The extent of his influence on decisions partly depended on the quality of his input. Furthermore he was being asked to become involved at a much earlier than normal stage and to have continuous involvement in planning, review and re-planning. His role as go-between and communicator between employees and management was still there, but is likely to be altered if more employees themselves become involved at some stage. Even without this, he is almost inevitably being asked to extend his inter-personal skills into the handling of group situations .... This change from a 'defensive' to a 'positive' role makes for greater demands on the individual steward and this will require acknowledgement from the management and greater support from the trade union.'[18]

These changes in the role of the shop-steward had implications also for the role of the branch secretary who because of his other commitments had to delegate to the shop-steward and, indeed, to the men, a part of his functions. Indeed, at the negotiation stage, the branch secretary was left with little more than a 'rubber-stamping' job to do. In this case, he was prepared to play the restricted role left to him although he was clearly not happy or at ease with it. What had happened was that the involvement of the men in the project had not only required the managers and specialists on the project team to devolve to the men certain activities normally reserved for management to determine, it had required a parallel process of devolution, on the part of the branch secretary, to the shop-steward and to the men. The process of devolution from the branch secretary to the shop-steward is of course no new phenomenon in this country extending back to the advent of plant bargaining in the early 1960s and, in some industries, well beyond that. It is easy to see though how the process could be accelerated through the extension of joint regulation in the factory to a much wider range of issues than pay and conditions. This points to a change in the relationship of the branch secretary to the shop-steward whereby the former, as Lovelady suggests, takes on more of a role of co-ordinator, policy-maker and organiser of his stewards. But this development raises questions about the traditional negotiating role of the branch secretary with some important implications for management. Lovelady comments on these as follows:

'Likewise, his negotiation role, though still a major priority, is different. A defensive line to prevent poor agreements is certainly required. But here, the branch secretary may be seen as a ratifier of local projects, bearing in mind the good of the whole branch as well as sectional interests. However, management must recognise the dangers to the whole organisation of pushing the secretary into a purely 'rubber-stamping' role. This is plainly a disadvantage since the branch secretary needs to be seen as effective to carry the membership with him. It is of no advantage to management, to deal with an unrepresentative representative.'[19]

We referred earlier to the reluctance displayed by many trade union officials to engage in joint regulation activities of a 'win-win' nature outside the traditional bargaining areas of pay and conditions. This is often matched by a reluctance to allow the membership to become inolved either. An extension of joint regulation on the lines that we have just described in the case above would appear to necessitate a re-examination of this attitude. If trade unions want managements to let go of the reins, then they may need to let go of the reins as well. Just as a full-time official cannot be everywhere at once, neither can a shop-steward so that an extension of joint regulation into issues such as work organisation and methods may only be possible where trade union officials are prepared to relax what many of them see as a monopoly position of work-force representation.

We have already laid emphasis on the responsibility of senior managements to help their subordinate managers acquire the skills and attitudes required as a consequence of extending joint regulation into areas of decision-making previously confined to management. Similarly, we see it as their responsibility to provide such help to their employee representatives. This is not to exonerate trade unions from any responsibility in this matter but there are three important reasons why managements should take the initiative in the learning of new attitudes and skills.

In the first place, companies are far better endowed than trade unions in terms of training know-how and resources.

Even the small and medium-sized firm with no established personnel or training function has nowadays wide access to relevant expertise through employers' associations, industrial training boards and higher education establishments.

Secondly, trade unionists are unlikely to see the relevance of new skills and attitudes unless managements create the framework within which they can be exercised. Trade unions by and large respond to and adapt to the way that managements behave; in the area of participation up to the present, management acts and trade unions react, rather than the other way round. Where managements have created a framework for employee representatives to play a greater role in joint regulation and have provided the training demanded, we see little or no evidence that representatives have, as it were, used the bullets to fire back at management.

Our third reason is that in-company training in which the training material consists of real issues and problems facing the employee representative in his day-to-day job provides the most powerful learning medium of all. The CIR Report on *Industrial Relations Training* points out that training to achieve improvements in industrial relations or to achieve change must take as its starting point an assessment of 'the situations in industrial relations where the needs occur'.[20] Experience, to be exploited to its full learning potential, needs to be supplemented by appropriate concepts and frames of reference which permit the experience to be reviewed and improvements and modifications to be incorporated into future behaviour. This sort of learning demands high calibre trainers able to work alongside shop stewards and other employees undertaking representative roles for periods of months or even years at a time, albeit not on an everyday basis, and it is doubtful that trade unions, even if they wanted to, would provide a training service of this sort given their present general level of resources and other commitments.

The onus therefore falls on managements to provide training. For managements so to do may give rise to suspicion at best and outright opposition at worst as far as many trade unionists are concerned. But again the evidence does not lead to the conclusion that where companies have taken the initiative in the training of employee representatives, the result is the creation of bosses' men. The outcome is rather a development of the role of the employee representative which, while it permits his involvement in areas of decision-making traditionally left to management, does not compromise but rather strengthens his negotiating function.

Participation and the employee

Running through the company submissions to the Bullock Committee was a very marked tendency to doubt whether employees were interested on the whole in further participation in decision-making. This viewpoint was only qualified to the extent that some companies stated that the demand for further participation on the part of their workers was confined to an interest on the one hand in having more information about company performance, plans and prospects and, on the other, in having more scope for involvement at the immediate place of work. Possibly with the terms of reference of the Bullock Committee in mind, with their emphasis on worker representation on boards of directors, most companies in their evidence made a point of casting very strong doubts indeed on whether employees were in any way interested in board level representation.

It can be argued that since the company evidence to Bullock was overwhelmingly originated by managers (only a handful of companies based their evidence on opinion surveys or audits), the evidence in effect reflects managers' perceptions of the views of employees rather than the views of employees themselves. Similarly one might ask how far the trade union submissions should be considered expressions of the views of the leadership rather than those of the rank and file. How far and in what ways do people want to participate in decisions that affect their lives and livelihoods, which affect the shape of their jobs and job environment?

One response to the question might be to cite evidence suggesting low levels of interest by workers in trade union matters – the relatively low penetration of trade unions in certain industries and among certain occupational groups, the low turn-outs at branch meetings, the low polls in ballots for union officials, the frequently uncontested and re-elections of shop stewards[21] – and conclude that where an opportunity is offered to workers to influence these decisions through what would seem an obvious vehicle, the trade unions, the opportunity does not appear to be taken up with anything like enthusiasm. But this line of argument ignores the question of what workers look for in trade unions and what they do not look for. It also does not take into account the evidence from a number of cases where, given the opportunity by management, and a framework to participate further in decisions affecting them, workers have responded in a positive way.

In our earlier discussion of the role of the employee representative *vis-à-vis* his members, we pointed out that the shop-floor tends to see the trade union almost as the institutionalised opposition to management. We further made the point that although workers see some of their interests as being opposed to those of management, they also see common interests as well. So that, while the union is seen as the means of protecting workers' interests insofar as they clash with those of management, the fact that it is cast in the role of opposition and fulfils expectations by behaving like an opposition means that it may not be seen by workers as the natural channel for promoting their

involvement in those matters where they perceive their
interests and those of management to be in accord. But
managers also tend to see the role of the union in a similar
way (i.e. as opposition) with the result that unions are put in
the position of finding it difficult to conceive of any role for
themselves beyond that of defending and promoting their
members' interests in the restricted areas of material
rewards and job security. So if workers do have a real desire
to participate more fully where they share common
interests with management, how can we know that this is
so; that given the scope to extend their involvement, they
will make use of it? We believe that it is only possible for
managers to get an answer to this question by providing
this scope. Workers are in a subordinate role to managers;
they cannot provide such scope for themselves.

As noted in Chapter 5, several researchers have found
relationships between these kinds of factor and the
effectiveness of participation. Certainly, as Goldthorpe's
findings suggest,[22] it would be naive to believe that all
employees are endowed with a latent desire to play a fuller
role in decision-making and to make available to their
employers hitherto untapped sources of talent. Nevertheless
our own consulting experience together with evidence from
cases such as the ICI Gloucester Plant leads us to the
conclusion that employees at all levels have much more to
contribute to the running of their companies than senior
management generally gives them credit for.

But certain conditions are necessary for this potential
contribution to be realised. First, senior management has to
recognise that it is there, rather than take refuge in slogans,
which are at best only partly true, to the effect that workers
simply want to be told what to do and leave managers to get
on with managing. Second, this contribution will not be
forthcoming unless workers are confident that their basic
security needs are being met and that they will be able to

share with their employers the rewards occurring from it. Third, where trade unions are recognised, managements should seek to work through them and provide the leadership and the training to help trade unionists develop the ability to play a creative, problem-solving role in addition to, (not instead of), their traditional role of opposing management in areas of conflicting interest. Fourth, there must be a recognition on management's part (and, indeed, on the part of everyone concerned), that the extension of employee involvement in decision-making requires time, hard effort and the ability to cope with a great many setbacks and frustrations.

On a final cautionary note, managers should beware of being deluded into the belief that through participation, employees will come to see things from management's point of view and that conflicts of interest will be diminished if not disappear altogether. Cases of successful participation in fields of common interest tend to build up a climate of trust and mutual goodwill that enable issues where interests conflict to be dealt with less acrimoniously. Nevertheless, although managements exercise a significant influence on the attitudes of their employees, other factors, both at work and outside, influence attitudes as well. Despite the impressive progress in extending participation achieved at Olsen throughout the late 1960s and early 1970s, the Olsen dockworkers joined subsequent dock strikes in the port. To point this out is not to diminish the Olsen achievement by any means. Nor do we believe that the decision by the Olsen dockworkers provides justification for the sceptical manager or trade unionist to take an 'I could have told you so' attitude. The lesson to be drawn is that employee involvement in areas of common interest with management can have a powerful impact on efficiency, communications, job satisfaction and the smoothness with which changes are carried out. But participation in this sense is no guarantee that when workers perceive an issue of conflict with management, they will not take a conflict stance.

References

1. George Strauss, 'Group Dynamics and Intergroup Relations', in W.F. Whyte, *Money and Motivation*, Harper and Row (London 1955), pp. 90–96.
2. *Ibid.*, p. 96.
3. *Ibid.*, p. 96.
4. See S. Cotgrove, J. Dunham, C. Vanplew, *The Nylon Spinners*, Allen and Unwin (London 1971), and W.W. Daniel and N. McIntosh, *The Right to Manage?*, Macdonald (London 1972).
5. For descriptions of the Olsen case see Lynda King Taylor, 'Participation without Patronising', *Industrial Commerical Training*, (May 1973), pp. 211–15; A. Coveney, 'Olsen's Democracy', *Industrial Society*, (Nov–Dec 1975), pp. 11–13; J. Wellens, *Worker Participation: a practical policy*, Wellens Publishing (Guilsborough 1975), pp. 43–52; and 'The Supervisor and Technological Change – A Study of the Changing Role of the Supervisor in the Port Transport Industry', *Occasional Papers No. 1*, National Ports Council, (London 1970).
6. F.J. Roethlisberger, 'The Foreman: Master and Victim of Double Talk', *Harvard Business Review*, Vol 23, (1945, pp. 285–94).
7. *Front Line Management*, British Institute of Management Working Party Report (London 1976).
8. W.H. Scott, *Industrial Leadership and Joint Consultation*, Liverpool University Press (Liverpool 1952), p. 165.
9. C. Argyris, *Personality and Organisation*, Harper and Row (New York 1957). The same point was noted empirically by Scott *op. cit.*, p. 104.

10. G.F. Thomason, *Experiments in Participation*, Institute of Personnel Management (London 1971), p. 47.

11. Evidence of the Electrical, Electronic, Telecommunication and Plumbing Union to the Bullock Committee. Quoted by the *Bullock Committee*, HMSO (London 1977), pp. 39–40.

12. Daniel and McIntosh, *op. cit.*, p. 123.

13. R.E. Walton and R.B. McKersie, *A Behavioral Theory of Labor Negotiations*, McGraw-Hill (New York 1965).

14. J.H. Goldthorpe, D. Lockwood, F. Bechhofer, J. Platt, *The Affluent Worker: Industrial Attitudes and Behaviour*, Cambridge University Press (Cambridge 1968), pp. 96–8.

15. Government Social Survey, *Workplace Industrial Relations*, HMSO (London 1968).

16. Our personal knowledge of the Baxi Company was supplemented by Lynda King Taylor in '*Not For Bread Alone*', Business Books Limited (London 1973), pp. 33–43.

17. We are grateful to Louise Lovelady for providing us with access to this case study. For further details see L. Lovelady 'Workplace Democratisation – Problems at the Union-Management Inter-face'. Paper prepared at the University of Salford for publication by the International Quality of Working Life Committee (forthcoming).

18. *Ibid.*

19. *Ibid.*

20. Commission on Industrial Relations, Report No. 33, *Industrial Relations Training*, HMSO (London 1972), p. 38.

21. See for example H.A. Clegg, A.J. Killick, R. Adams, *Trade Union Officers*, Blackwell (Oxford 1961).

22. Goldthorpe *et al, op. cit.*

8 Skills of Participation

Introduction

A marked feature of the debate on participation and industrial democracy, which has been going on in the United Kingdom since the setting up of the Bullock Committee, and indeed before then, has been the overwhelming concern with the structural and procedural aspects. Attention has been largely focussed on issues such as should there be a single- or a two-tier board of directors, how should employee representatives be appointed or elected, what restrictions should there be on the disclosure of information by employee representatives to their constituents and what provision should be made for boards to report back to shareholders?

By comparison, there has been little attention paid to the question of what help people need in order to cope with changes brought about within their companies through the extension of employee involvement in decision-making, what problems of adjustment they are likely to face, what new skills and attitudes they will need to learn and how training can contribute. This is unfortunate because, while no organisation, however participative or otherwise, can operate without at least a minimum of structures and procedures, it is not so much these that determine the success or otherwise of experiments in participation, but the underlying philosophies and value systems of the organisation, the climate of human relationships and the skills that people have for handling these relationships. No amount of tinkering with board structures, election procedures and committee terms of reference can bring about participation. People will only make participation work if they are both able and willing to make it work. We said at the beginning of Chapter 6 that participation involves far more than simply introducing new procedures and institutions into organisations without significantly affecting their way of life. You cannot, as it were, introduce participation and expect to carry on as before.

This reasoning leads us to believe that the major contribution of training as far as participation is concerned lies in helping in the development of attitudes and skills appropriate to a pattern of decision-making that involves more people than it did previously. This is not to say that learning about relevant legislation, company policy and procedures, and the financial side of business are unimportant. If people are expected to make relevant contributions on any aspect of the business, they need to know what they are talking about and, if necessary, training should be provided. But the really difficult training issues in participation are not about how do we get employee representatives to understand a balance sheet, how do we introduce new safety representatives to the Health and Safety at Work Act, or how do we help our pension fund trustees learn about how the company invests the funds. They are much more complex than issues such as these.

For example, how do you help managers accustomed over a lifetime to making decisions with a minimum of shop-floor consultation get used to the idea of having to consult with people whose contributions they may up to now have largely ignored? What issues should be opened up to wider consultation anyway and how much is being risked in doing so? How do you ensure that representatives really do represent? How do you help trade unionists who see their role purely in bargaining terms, acquire skills of creative problem-solving and, more important, be

prepared to put them into practice? What do you do about
the fact that many employees appear to be quite apathetic
about participation and resist all attempts to involve them
in decision-making? How do you help managers and
employee representatives adjust to having to operate in a
much more exposed way than they have been used to?
Training for participation is very much to do with helping
people overcome deep-seated anxieties and fears. Unless it
can do this, it will fail.

Training for participation that concentrates on skill
acquisition only (e.g. taking part in meetings, representing
the views of others) will not go far enough; it must also give
practical help and encouragement in such a way that
learners will see the relevance of the skills to their jobs and
be motivated to apply them. This will be helped if the
training clearly has top management support even to the
extent that top management is involved in the training
process itself. Such training and, indeed, participation itself,
needs to be kept in the mainstream of organisational life if
it is to retain its credibility and have any impact on
organisational performance or individual perceptions. Such
training, furthermore, should wherever possible be job-
related. Academic courses have their place in the total
picture, but they will be effective in advancing participation
to the extent that they can be related by course members to
their specific job situation. Once a basic appreciation has
been obtained, every effort should be made to conduct
training in their application in the practical job settings
concerned. Such practical job settings should be tied to a
broad training programme which permits both a frequent
application of the lessons learned and a time for reflection
and feedback to the training group on particular
experiences.

We see three key areas of training for participation:
training in teamwork skills, training in skills of
representation, and support training. By the latter we mean
training aimed at developing styles of management and a

climate of relations that are in harmony with and promote participation. We suggest that each of these areas of training is necessary for the total participation we referred to in the earlier chapters. Each is necessary also for participation at any one level be it board level, middle range or participation at the level of the job itself.

Teamwork skills

Most managers in our experience find working in groups one of the less satisfactory and less satisfying parts of their job. Groups, meetings, councils and committees tend to be associated with feelings of boredom, frustration and insecurity; they seem to waste a great deal of time in comparison with the results that they achieve. We more than suspect that herein lies much of the cynicism that managers and others express about participation – that it means still further meetings in a schedule already dominated by meetings. The problem, however, is that group activities are inescapable in organisations nowadays. Demands by employees for a higher level of participation in decision-making in recent years have only given extra weight to the trend whereby increasing size, diversity and complexity in organisations have combined to make decision-making more and more a function that is at least prepared for, if not carried out, by groups rather than individuals. If decision-making by groups or teams is to become increasingly a feature of life in organisations, then the challenge is how to make groups more effective. What do we mean by an effective group? Lippitt and Seashore sum up the characteristics of an effective group as follows:

'Successful group productivity depends on the ability of the members to exchange ideas freely and clearly, and to feel involved in the decisions and processes of the group.

'A collection of capable individuals does not always

produce a capable group. Mature adults often form an immature working team. When people get together, they assume a character and existence all their own, growing into a mature working group or becoming infantile in their handling of problems. A number of investigations are now studying this area of group pathology, identifying reasons why some groups fail to be creative and productive.

'Groups may be helped to grow to maturity; they need not develop like Topsy. By using appropriate procedures, groups can become more productive, channel energies into effective work and eliminate or replace internal conflicts that block group progress. The ability of a group to function properly is not necessarily dependent on the leader. No group can become fully productive until its members are willing to assume responsibility for the way the group acts. Any group can benefit from a skilled leader, but to get creative group thinking, group decisions, and group actions, many different roles are required. The effective leader must realise, (and help the members to realise), that each member must contribute to the total task of leadership.'[1]

Training can contribute to improving effectiveness in two main ways. First, it can help at a conceptual level in terms of developing an understanding of how groups work. Second, it can help at a practical level in terms of developing the skills to apply this understanding. In the same way that an engineer exercises his skills within the framework of various concepts, models and principles to do with the properties of the materials and machines with which he works, we believe that effective group work also demands frameworks of understanding to enable group members better to relate their choice of structure and methods to the task of the group, to select skills appropriate to the particular needs of the group at any one time, and to provide a means of reviewing group performance and planning improvements.

One such framework is described in Figure 8.1 It illustrates four balances that a group has to maintain to work effectively. These balances are:

1. Data giving and data handling Groups require data, information, ideas and opinions as the raw materials on which they work. To make sense of this raw material however and to achieve the most efficient usage, groups also require means of handling it. At stages in group work where the input or generation of data is all-important, the group needs a loose structure and an uncritical frame of mind so as not to inhibit the flow of data. However, to ensure that none of the data gets lost, the group will need to decide beforehand on a means of recording or classifying the data. A classic failing of groups is not that they are short on ideas and relevant information; it is just that they take insufficient trouble to handle it. But conversely there is a danger that too heavy an emphasis on the data handling side of the balance (e.g. heavy-handed chairmanship, rigid adherence to rules and procedures) will impair creativity and the inflow of data.

2. Initiating behaviour and mediating behaviour Initiating behaviour is associated with opening lines such as 'How about .... ? 'Why don't we .... ?' 'If you ask me I think we should .... ,' 'What we need to do now is .... ' Groups need behaviour of this sort to get movement, to breathe life into them, to spark them off. But they also need behaviour of a mediating type which is to do with encouraging other people's opinions, attempting to harmonise different points of view, suggesting ways out of disagreements, summarising the feelings and mood of the group. Too many initiatives produces a group rather like a runaway horse with plenty of

Figure 8.1   Balances in Effective Teamwork

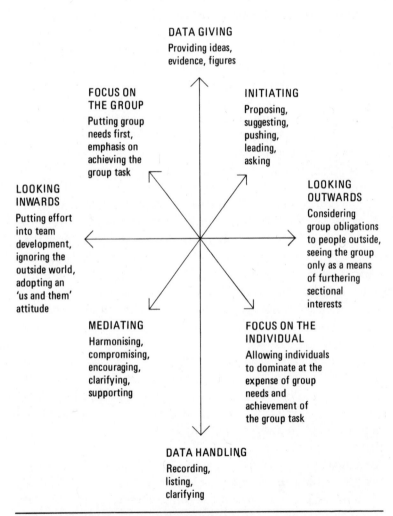

DATA GIVING
Providing ideas,
evidence, figures

FOCUS ON
THE GROUP
Putting group
needs first,
emphasis on
achieving the
group task

INITIATING
Proposing,
suggesting,
pushing,
leading,
asking

LOOKING
INWARDS
Putting effort
into team
development,
ignoring the
outside world,
adopting an
'us and them'
attitude

LOOKING
OUTWARDS
Considering
group obligations
to people outside,
seeing the group
only as a means
of furthering
sectional
interests

MEDIATING
Harmonising,
compromising,
encouraging,
clarifying,
supporting

FOCUS ON THE
INDIVIDUAL
Allowing individuals
to dominate at the
expense of group
needs and
achievement of
the group task

DATA HANDLING
Recording,
listing,
clarifying

energy and momentum but lacking in direction. Too many mediators on the other hand and the outcome is likely to be a pleasant comfortable atmosphere but with little to show by way of results.

3. Focus on the group and focus on the individuals Sometimes one encounters in groups such a high concern for achieving the group task that the particular needs, feelings and opinions of its individual members, (or some of them), are quite trampled on or ignored in the process. The expression of feelings within the group may be positively discouraged. On the other hand, the achievement of group tasks or the achievement of decisions which can be considered to be genuine reflections of group opinion, can be frustrated by one or a few dominant individuals who may be so unconsciously, because they have a tendency to talk too much for example or who deliberately use their status or power to steamroller the group.

4. Looking inwards and looking outwards Effective teamwork depends very much on a group's ability to build up a sense of identity, shared goals and standards that give it a uniqueness within the organisation. If members see themselves mainly as representing a particular interest or point of view and see their job as simply to defend and promote that interest at the expense of the interests of other members if necessary, or at the expense of the interests of the group, that sense of identity will not emerge. But groups can also develop this sense of identity to the point where they live in a world of their own, where the members become remote from their constituents and departments which they are representing, with the result that an unhealthy relationship develops with the organisation as a whole.

Using a framework of this sort, a group can assess how well it is working – its good points and its bad points.

Individual members can do their own assessments and then discuss it with other group members. Doing this however can be nothing more than an academic exercise unless the group, having highlighted its weaknesses and strengths, goes on to plan some action to improve and build on them. A trainer or observer who is not a member of the group, or a group member who has been asked to take on the role of observer, can be most valuable in helping the group review its performance by giving it feedback on what he has seen or heard. The observer's job is to act as a mirror to the group, not as a judge. He must reflect back to the group what he has seen and heard and describe the effect that it had on him. His observations must be accurate and to the point. Perhaps most of all they must be timed well. We are describing a role which demands a high level of trust from the group and a high level of sensitivity. It is also a role where an important criterion of success is how quickly the occupant can work himself out of a job so that the group members themselves take on the full responsibility for self-improvement.

How can self-improvement become built-in to a group? In the first place, members must want to make continuous self-improvement part of the way of life of the group and must be prepared to spend some time on it. One of the common characteristics of successful problem solving groups is that they devote time to reviewing and planning in a conscious manner, realising that improvement will not just happen but rather has to be made to happen. What they are thus doing in effect is carrying out their work on the basis of the cycle in Figure 8.2.

During the planning phase of the cycle, group members try to get agreement on where they are going, what they are trying to achieve and the criteria for evaluating success. They discuss working methods, who is going to do what, whether or not a leader should be appointed, what resources are available to the group in terms of time, know-how,

Figure 8.2   The Improvement Cycle in Team Development

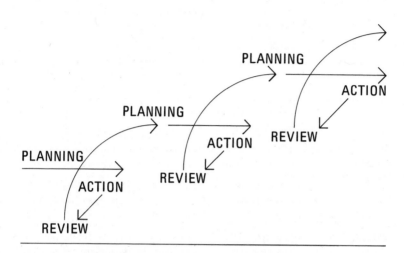

information. The temptation for any problem solving group is to dive straight into the action phase without doing any planning or skimping it with the result that time gets wasted, resources are under-utilised or not even recognised and people are confused about what the group is trying to do.

Most of the time that problem solving groups spend together is in the action phase, dealing with the job that the group has been given to do, designing a job evaluation scheme, revising a plant layout, drawing up a new factory disciplinary procedure or whatever. As a group becomes more skilled, generally the less time it needs to devote to planning periods and review periods.

In the review phase, the group is asking itself the question 'how are we doing?' This may include a discussion as to whether the group is on course to its long-term goals, how well it is using its time and how appropriate are its methods. Some groups prefer unstructured approaches to reviewing their performance. Others find it useful to work to a framework such as the one set out in Figure 8.1. But

whichever approach is used, it must lead to a further
planning phase which specifies improvements to be aimed
for (e.g. 'We'll try to keep better track of our time by asking
Jim to tell us every time fifteen minutes are up', or 'Let's
make a special effort from now on to keep our mouths shut
while other people are talking'). Thus the cycle begins
again.

We noted in our study of the key features of a
participation steering group in Chapter 6 that leadership in
a group can take two forms: leadership based on relevant
know-how to do with the topic under consideration and
leadership to do with management of the task procedure.
This second form of leadership is to do with helping a group
work through the improvement cycle that we have just
outlined. It involves taking the initiative in the group
particularly in the planning phase and the review phase.
The leader can also help in setting and maintaining the pace
of work, by being particularly conscious of and helping the
group to maintain a dynamic balance in terms of the four
axes in Figure 8.1 and ensuring that the group lives up to
the standards that it sets itself for its behaviour. Such a
leader must be able to work in a consultative style allowing
the group to exercise a large proportion of its own
leadership in the task procedure sense.

Team development only begins to happen when team
members become committed to the idea and are prepared
to take concrete steps to do something about it.

But the organisation outside can help as well. First, it can
try to ensure that problem solving groups are well balanced
in terms of the particular strengths, personalities and
experience of the members chosen. This is worth some time
and care but we should note that it is the very antithesis of
selection on the basis of crude formulas based on equal
representation from the management side and the
employees' side or representation in proportion to
numbers employed by department. Second, as in the case of

the participation steering group, problem solving groups must have the backing of management and employees through their collective representation. Third, groups, unless they have only a short life of (say) less than six months, can be helped to keep in touch with the rest of the company through a rotation of members.

It might be asked 'how can groups of the sort just described ever work when they are composed of managers and employees who have been used to a relationship based on conflict and bargaining?' The answer is that they *can* work and *do* work as we describe in Chapter 7. But to work they require leadership and a willingness to make them work on the part of people of key influence in the company such as senior managers and employee representatives.

Skills of representation

In small concerns where everyone is in day-to-day contact with each other, participation in decision-making can take place without having representatives. But once numbers reach a certain point, the organisation begins to differentiate in the way that we described in Chapter 5. The process happens in two ways: it happens vertically in the sense of the emergence of defined functions and specialisms and laterally through the development of a hierarchy of authority. The process of differentiation needs to be balanced by some means of co-ordinating what goes on in the various parts and at the various levels of the organisation. One of the chief means of achieving co-ordination is through people who are given the titles of manager and supervisor.

Managers and supervisors, like Janus, the Roman deity, face both ways. They are part of the authority or executive system of the organisation in that they have the job of implementing policies and decisions made by their superiors. But they are representatives of their plants, function, departments and the people who work in them as well, even though this concept may seem somewhat novel to some of them. So a manager or supervisor can be a representative in just the same way as someone who is elected by employees to represent them. And where there are no elected representatives, the manager or supervisor is the only formal channel of representation, which makes it important that besides being good at managing or supervising in the sense of getting things done, he also pays attention to his responsibilities in representing the interests of his subordinates. In fact, when employees decide to elect their *own* representative from among their numbers, this is typically a response to a perception on their part that management is failing to represent their interests adequately.

In the same way that meetings, committees and working parties tend to arouse cynical reactions as inefficient media for decision-making, the concept of representation also gives rise to cynicism. People express cynicism not only about the way in which employee representatives and trade unions do their job but about their representatives in central and local government as well. Representatives are criticised for failing to consult the people whom they represent, so that the way in which representation is exercised is seen as a function of the opinions and biases of the representative rather than a synthesis of the viewpoints of his constituents.

Representation is seen by some as a game in which success is a matter of bluff and counter-bluff together with a mastery of how to use rules and procedures to one's own advantage. It is also seen, and perhaps this is encouraged by the assumptions underlying the two-party system in Parliament, as synonymous with opposition. Daniel and McIntosh attribute part of the reason for workers' apathy towards their unions to a perception on their part that 'all it does is oppose';[2] it does not play a creative and constructive role in decision-making but sees itself as the opposition to management in the sense of a parliamentary opposition.

All this may be to paint an unduly gloomy picture of representation in action and perhaps there is a widespread tendency to undervalue the contributions made by people who carry out various representative roles in our society and to be parsimonious in our appreciation. Nevertheless, as participation is extended as a way of life in organisations, the role of the representative becomes even more important. Representatives are rather like filters and valves in a living organism; if the filters get clogged up and the valves fail, then the organism breaks down. So good representation, like good teamwork, is vital for good participation.

We distinguish between representation and delegation. At times of crisis representatives may be seen to be mandated to take a particular view. But this is not the normal role of the representative. He is not delegated to carry a specific vote. He is chosen to represent a broad sweep of interests and the extent to which he can do this will depend as much on his personal qualities as on the structural arrangements that have been agreed. The choice of a representative in terms of his personal qualities rather than as a mouth-piece for a set position makes considerable demands on the individual. Perhaps most important of these is that he maintains a close relationship with his 'constituents', that he reports back regularly and does not develop a set of private interests as 'representative' which divorce him from the body of workers. We saw one way in which this danger was being consciously avoided in the Granges Weda foundry at Upplands Vasby described in Chapter 4.* Concentrating representation on the more highly skilled 'first man' proved unsatisfactory for the remainder of the casters. They then moved to a scheme

---

*See p. 114 above.

which included casters as representatives and introduced rotation of representation. The ultimate aim of the fully participative organisation will not be achieved by mechanically establishing an additional cadre of professional representatives seeking eventually to protect their own position and providing a barrier between worker and management rather than a channel.

Training can contribute to the quality of representation by role analysis and through the development of specific skills of representation. Let us look at role analysis first. To do his job well, any representative needs to be clear about what is expected of him. This is never an easy task for those who have the job of intermediary, broker or go-between and who need to be sensitive all the time to changes in the situation surrounding their job, changes in people's moods and the way they see their priorities and changes in the delicate balances of power and influence. Role analysis is a tool to develop and maintain this sort of sensitivity. There are a number of techniques for learning how to use role analysis which, we should add, is of relevance as a tool not only to representatives as such but to people generally whose job success depends critically on how they work with and through others. What role analysis is designed to do then for the representative is to sharpen his awareness of the critical aspects that go to make up his role so that he is better able to adjust to the changing demands on his role. By critical aspects, we mean:

1. *Uniqueness*

   What can I uniquely contribute as a representative because of:

   – my skills, knowledge, experience?

   – my position in the company, status, point of view?

– the relationships that I have within the company?

2. *Expectations*

What do the people whom I am representing expect of me?

What do other representatives with whom I have contact expect of me?

Do I feel the need to try to modify these expectations? How?

3. *Constraints*

What are the constraints on my job as representative? (e.g. lack of time, lack of secretarial support, misunderstanding of my job)

Which of these constraints:

– are irremovable?

– can other people help me to do something about?

– can I begin to do something about?

4. *Needs and Priorities*

What are my priorities as a representative?

What timings or targets are practical?

How should I tackle them?

5. *Activities and use of time*

What should I therefore be doing now?

How should I be using my time?

It should be pointed out that role analysis is not a once-and-for-all activity that a representative should carry out on taking up the job and then forget about. On the contrary, it should be practiced to the point where it comes to be carried out almost unconsciously.

Turning now to the specific skills of representation, we see these as being grouped under three main headings: receiving communications, giving communications and monitoring decisions.

Receiving communications demands good listening ability so that not only the words are heard but also the underlying message or meaning. It demands the ability to see balances and syntheses in the viewpoints that people are presenting and skill in the use of questions to check with people what they are communicating. Important too is being aware of one's own values and prejudices, keeping these in the background and not making premature judgments.

In giving communications, the representative has to blend the views of a number of people into one agreed view, to present what he has to say in an understandable and acceptable way and check that what he has said has been understood. He must be sensitive in his choice of time and situation when communicating.

In order to monitor decisions that representatives have made together, each needs to be clear and in agreement with the others as to what decisions have in fact been taken, what action is to be taken and by whom in consequence of these decisions. Monitoring, then, requires that representatives decide on criteria for assessing the implementation of the decisions and make arrangements for following up action to be taken and to ensure that the real intentions behind the decisions are in fact carried out.

Companies can ensure that the representative function works well in a number of ways. First, they can take steps to see that representatives are given training. Second, they can provide time and, where necessary, secretarial support to enable representatives to play a full role. We see no advantage to any company in the long-term in having representatives who are poorly trained and ill-equipped to represent. Third, representation needs a structure in which to operate, which must be based on the key 'building blocks' which make up the company. A structure can be based on departments, functions or specialist groupings or some combination of each. The unique circumstances of each company mean that no two representative structures can be completely alike but certain criteria are essential whatever the structure adopted. First, representatives must be clear about what their roles are within the structure. This is where role analysis can contribute. Similarly, the roles of representative bodies, (e.g. the works council, departmental productivity teams, the safety committee, must also be clearly stated and publicised whether they are permanent or temporary. How they relate to each other also needs to be clarified (e.g. the procedure whereby the works council appoints members to the pensions committee, what issues are dealt with at factory level *vis-à-vis* those dealt with by participative machinery at departmental level).

The structure, too, must be seen as acceptable and fair so that every member of the company can feel that he is adequately represented through it. Last, to avoid a nightmare of meetings and papers, the structure should be designed to make decisions to be carried out as close to the point of implementation as possible, where most knowledge of the issues involved lies.

Support training for participation

Participation, if it is to work effectively, needs a company environment that is in sympathy with its underlying philosophies. However much a company may invest in training in teamwork and representational skills for those directly involved in participative activities, it will only reap full benefit from its investment providing that it takes steps also to encourage a climate and management style that are in tune with the philosophies on which these activities are based. This means taking every opportunity to build into people's jobs as much challenge, scope for exercising discretion and involvement in decisions affecting them, as they can competently and willingly handle. In terms of management style, it means moving away from decision-making without consultation towards decision-making through consultation and co-decision.

This is not to say that a participative style of management requires every single decision to be made only after consultation. Some decisions are of such complexity that it is probably best to let one person handle them alone and that person may well be the manager. In a crisis or when a decision is needed quickly, there may not be time for consultation so that the manager must act on his own. What we are saying is that the way in which a decision is made should depend on the situation. Sometimes the needs of the task to be done will take precedence, at other times, the needs of the people concerned. What the manager has to do is maintain a running balance between the two sets of needs.

Doubt and discussion about whether particular decisions should have been 'co-determined' or referred to one group or another may well characterise the early days of participation. But as participative practice matures in a company such concerns should feature less. If participation is ever to be more than a collection of committees, it must foster the growth of trusting relationships and the extent of such relationships, though difficult to measure, are, in our view, the ultimate criterion of successful participation. In such an environment managers, supervisors, employees, shop-stewards can be trusted on occasion to take unilateral decisions because the situation demanded it. In such an environment it will be 'natural' to act in a way consistent with the entire thrust of earlier discussions and to report back on action taken at the earliest occasion possible. In such an environment it would not be expected that the company should miss an opportunity because the necessary people could not be convened. Building such an environment is the task of each participative 'incident'; it is also the task of 'support training'.

Many companies have in recent years embarked on programmes designed to develop more participative or consultative styles of management. These programmes are usually based on the insights and research of behavioural scientists such as Tannenbaum, Likert and McGregor.[3] Managers are introduced to a range of alternative management styles, helped to identify their own preferred style through questionnaires and/or group activities and also given help in choosing and practicing styles appropriate to different situations.

An important part of such support training may be described under the general heading of 'sensitivity training'. This involves developing a greater level of self-understanding, of understanding of others and of understanding the processes of group interaction through which behaviour is manifested. In the past such forms of training have been conducted outside the company and the anonymity afforded by such neutral settings has been seen as a positive advantage in the training process. We would suggest, however, that if such training is to produce a new company style, there is a limit to the effectiveness of such out-company activity. The important focus of such training should be the development of a new sub-culture based on improved inter-personal understanding and new organisational norms in the matter of communications, co-ordination and decision-making. Although there will inevitably be strains and embarrassments at times, it is our experience that substantial advantages can accrue if such support training brings outside consultants to the organisation rather than taking individual managers to outside courses.

Group training to these ends is only one form that the

process of establishing a new organisational style may take. The process is inextricably bound to the question of management development. Counselling, coaching and setting objectives are parts of such a development process which can all be used for the development of a new organisational style supportive of participation.

But this process cannot be hurried. It is a long-term process which requires continuing support and confidence from the most senior levels. It is interesting in this respect to examine the histories of companies with a successful record in the field. A large number of them are characterised by a continuity of management philosophy over many years. The John Lewis Partnership, ICI, Scott Bader or Volvo, for example, illustrate this point.

A contrary situation was found in a firm studied by the authors. Here a series of mergers between family firms in the 1960s had brought together companies with quite different management styles. After the merger, autocratic 'hire and fire' management coexisted with a benevolently, paternalistic group. Each set kept to its original plants and a dual managing directorship overcame the problem of which group had ultimate formal power. Not surprisingly, this hybrid did not prosper. It was later taken over by a multinational with a reputation for a professional, participative management style. The multinational attempted to imprint its style on the whole enterprise by ending the joint managing directorship and moving its own nominees into this and other key directorships. More than a year later, however, the newly appointed personnel director recognised that the firm had still a lot of ground to cover if it was to achieve a uniform style which was participative in character.

This company had begun to move in this direction quite rapidly by establishing sympathetic managers in key positions at the top and by establishing a programme of management development throughout the organisation.

This programme enabled the senior management to bring forward young men who were not yet set in the older behavioural patterns. But the new company had not solved the problem of how to reconcile deeply entrenched and firmly held views and philosophies among middle-management.

The case illustrates a number of points. Firstly, the present situation is an out-growth of former situations which cannot now be influenced. So at a given moment organisations will vary in their training needs and their readiness for participation. Secondly, the development of a supportive management style is a long-term process calling for resources of resilience and faith as well as money. Finally, and a development of this, elements may well be inherited in a situation which make it quite impossible to progress until a fundamental change has been achieved in the situation.

In a further company known to the authors, a take-over resulted in the former company secretary inheriting the post of deputy managing director. It was quickly realised that this appointment had been a mistake as the person was totally opposed to the company style being developed by the new team. It was mutually agreed that this person would take a sideways move into a position little affected by the changes underway. The move was achieved without damaging the individual's self-respect or standing in the firm and resulted in benefit for all parties.

But if, as in the case described above, there is not one man but a significant part of the management hierarchy opposed to the developments, senior management may have little choice other than to bide their time and plan succession arrangements with care. Furthermore the issues raised in Chapter 5 about the appropriateness of different styles require close consideration before irrevocable decisions affecting human relationships are embarked upon.

Guidelines for effective training

Effective training is training that meets a need. The training carried out by any company therefore should reflect whatever its intentions are in developing participation, its plans for realising these intentions and the pace that it sets itself. We referred in Chapter 6 to how a training specialist can contribute to getting training for participation under way – advising on where to begin, on learning objectives and learning methods and so on – but we also made the point that training for participation must sooner rather than later become 'owned' by the people in the company so that *they* take responsibility for it – not the training specialist. So training expertise may be used but steps must be taken for the skills of the training specialist to be passed on. One way of doing this is for the training specialist to develop a small group of people – managers and employee representatives, perhaps, who are members of the steering group – to become trainers themselves in participation-related skills who gradually take over from the training specialist and can be released from their normal jobs from time to time to help others learn their skills.

The skills of participation like any others are best learnt and developed by practice on the job; so while there is an argument for learning initially to take place off-the-job so that learners can concentrate without distraction on acquiring basic skills, learning is only complete once the skills can be applied effectively on the job. Learning through the medium of the job requires some means of getting feedback on performance. Again, a training specialist can help by sitting in on groups and meetings and giving feedback but 'owning' participation means that people must devise and use their own feedback mechanisms (e.g. making a practice of building planning and reviewing periods into group activities) so that learning about participation becomes self-generating. It is certainly a mistake to think of training for participation as a once-and-for-all activity requiring a big push after which everyone can sit back and relax.

The theme of this chapter is well summarised in the words of a manager at Fred Olsen in discussion with John Wellens.

'It is real training this. And it certainly is a form of education. Actually we did consider sending foremen óut on courses but we became rather cynical. We could, for instance, have chosen a dozen courses and more on labour relations and human relations. But none of them seemed to have relevance to our situation. There were lectures on human relations but we had a real problem of human relations here in our own company. Why go away to study an academic case study when we have a real problem here to solve, where we know all the issues and all the characters and their funny little ways. You know what happens on a course. A chap goes away for a week or two. He absorbs all sorts of principles. But when he goes back he returns to one of these situations where nothing happens or can happen. We have learned a lot about these no-happen situations in our weekly meetings. They don't get the chance to put into operation the principles they have absorbed.

'Here we are training on the ground. We might make a real mess of it. But we soon find out and we hurry back to our little room and work out what we did wrong. It's marvellous! You have made a mistake but you have made progress: you know one way that is wrong. We have tried one solution we thought would work, it doesn't, scrub it, try again but always on a basis of frankness, co-operation, discussion and respect for the other man's point of view. As we do this we are all learning, managers, superintendents, foremen and workmen. You have the feeling that what you are doing is for real.'[4]

This distils the essence of training for participation. It must be firmly grounded in reality, using real (i.e. relevant and actually recognisable) issues and the people who were actually involved. It must link the learning with application. Learning in the real situation permits all parties to share the experience and this experience thus lends further support to the conflict of the learning. Because it is a common experience, it accelerates the recognition of common values fundamental to the whole process of participation and fosters a mutual tolerance during the inevitable set-backs in the long haul to effective participation.

References

1. G.L. Lippitt and E.W. Seashore, 'The Leader Looks at Group Effectiveness', *Looking into Leadership Monographs*, Leadership Resources Inc. (Washington DC, 1961), p. 1.
2. W.W. Daniel and N. McIntosh, *The Right to Manage?*, Macdonald (London 1972), p. 124.
3. A.S. Tannenbaum, *Control in Organisations*, McGraw-Hill (New York 1968); R. Likert, *New Patterns of Management*, McGraw-Hill (New York 1961); D. McGregor, *The Human Side of Enterprise*, McGraw-Hill (New York 1960).
4. J. Wellens, *Worker Participation: a Practical Policy*, Wellens Publishing (Guilsborough 1975), pp. 48-9.

9 Converging themes: some continuities and contradictions

The debate on participation is a continuing one and in such a situation it would be inappropriate to present 'conclusions'. In this chapter we shall draw together the various trends that have been discussed throughout the book and examine their implications for the development of participative styles of management. At the risk of appearing arbitrary, we have selected four interrelated themes as follows,

1. Participation is a concept applying to the total organisation.
2. Participation is aimed at establishing new relationships as well as new structures.
3. Participation is a managed process calling for a policy and a sense of overall direction.
4. Participation varies as organisations vary. There will be differential pressures calling for it and alternative means and opportunities to introduce it.

All of these themes, and many others, have appeared and re-appeared throughout the book. We draw them together here because of the way they interrelate with each other and thus usefully summarise what has been the main message we have wished to convey.

We have noted on several occasions that participation must be a total organisational activity. The decision hierarchy presented in Chapter 1 has provided a useful framework for examining the different levels of participative activity, but we do not wish to imply that such a framework should be applied rigidly and in all circumstances. The very antithesis of our conception of participation would be a series of demarcation disputes over where one hierarchical level of participation began and another left off. We do use the framework, however, to suggest the way in which participation should become an all-pervasive force in organisations.

Organisations, whether in industry or commerce, in health, educational or social services, should be seen as social systems. By this we mean that as collections of people, they have structure and form. They comprise parts and sub-parts and these parts interrelate. The parts which make the whole may be formally designated, or informally by the people themselves. Introduction of a major change – particularly a social change of the kind participation represents – cannot be confined to one part without affecting the others.

Again, a word of caution should be sounded. As we note below, participation is not equally applicable everywhere. It is not equally applicable from one organisation to the next nor is it equally applicable in all parts of the same organisation. But the 'total organisation' concept does not imply that it is.

For participation to apply to the total organisation it should be operative at every level in a way that allows the membership to appreciate its degree of application in different circumstances. In seeing participation as a total concept in this way, we must emphasise the way in which we see participation as being about relationships as well as structures.

It is when the idea of participation is seen in these terms that the need for a total organisational concept becomes clearer. It is possible to wear one mask when talking to non-participative department X, and a quite different mask involving different values and attitudes and behaviour when talking to highly participative department Y – but it is not satisfactory. When participation affects relationships it becomes difficult to switch on and off as one moves from department to department.

Difficulties arise particularly when the departments concerned attempt to talk to each other directly or when they are required to work closely together, when the different philosophies meet on committees and working parties or simply when they observe each other as they walk past their offices, drawing rooms and laboratories.

If participation were only a matter of structures – of voting, of constituencies, of meetings, minutes and agendas – then it might be reasonably contained within one department or one division. However, if participation is more than this, and we believe it must be, if it involves new attitudes and responsibilities, new definitions of objectives and methods of achieving them, new relationships between peers and between managers and men, then it cannot easily be contained.

For participation to achieve any change in behaviour in a permanent way, it must amend attitudes. Where we have found participation working, we have found a relationship that is based on mutual respect and which generates trust and confidence. If this is successfully achieved it cannot operate permanently only behind the walls of a single department or group of departments. It must be affected by and involve superiors up the line who are eventually responsible for both participative and non-participative departments. In this way, as well as by direct contact, all parts of the organisation will necessarily be brought into the process. But equally, where such trust relationships pervade the organisation, the operation of participation need not be mechanistically equal in all sections. Provided that confidence has been established and is not betrayed, different departments in the organisation may satisfactorily operate different participative forms. Indeed, effective operation probably requires that they do.

The concept of participation as pervading the total organisation in the form of new relationships rather than just new structures helps resolve two further difficulties with which we have been concerned. The middle management problem is eased. It becomes a problem only when structures are established through which representatives of lower levels by-pass middle levels when they participate with senior levels. Participation that emphasises new forms of relationship and norms of behaviour that permit lateral communications based on ability to contribute, cannot isolate any group simply because of its formal position. On the contrary, it is successful only in as much as it can involve expertise from any appropriate source. Middle management is an important source of organisational expertise and any participative system that promotes more organic forms must ultimately assist a middle management which can adapt and use appropriate leadership styles.

Participation in this way avoids the deadening possibility that it becomes an alternative bureaucracy. Representative democracy that fails to get past constitutional procedures will serve to maintain the distance between senior management and lower level members. An emphasis on primary groups, on rotation of membership in representation groups, on widespread training and involvement will help break down the institutionalisation of conflict and will spread the sense of ownership of the participative ideal.

When we talk of participation as a total organisational concept concerned with relationships rather than with structures, we cannot assume that left alone it will just happen. Participation, we have noted, needs to be managed. Such management should be a joint affair involving several different parties but it will contain a number of key features. There will be a policy regarding participation and thus a sense of direction. There will be support from the very top for what is not just a localised gimmick but an entire organisational philosophy.

It might be argued that participation is going to happen anyway and that organisations need only await the arrival of the legislation and then take the steps necessary to meet the legal requirements.

Such a policy, we suggest, would be short-sighted and produce a quite different result from that advocated here. Legislation can only apply to the structural features of participation. One cannot legislate for improved relationships and higher levels of confidence. Organisations that await the imposition of legal requirements in this area can expect to suffer all the inconvenience that the structural aspects of participation will bring in their wake without the positive benefits that can flow from the changed inter-personal climate.

A major reason for the development of clear policy on the question of participation is the way in which organisations vary in their need for participation and in the kind of participation that is appropriate and in the most suitable way in which it is to be introduced.

Legislation is necessarily a blunderbuss approach to the subject. It may make broad distinctions – for example, applying only to firms over a given size – but it cannot be finely attuned to particular needs. Organisations with an interest in participation will have their own starting points and their own 'image of the future'. It will take time to move towards this and there will be set-backs. These are easier to bear if there is a total sense of direction. Environmental change is a continuing process to which adaptation is easier in the light of total strategic policies.

The alternative is that the organisation drifts with regard to participation. It moves first in one direction in response to one pressure, and then in another direction in response to another pressure. Participation, however, is about human relationships. It cannot be installed overnight and taken away when the fashion changes. In affecting human relationships, it is a one-way process. Tom Lupton has described it as 'Pandora's box' and once it has been opened we cannot return to the former position.

In establishing a policy for participation and in assessing their situation, organisations should have regard for their external environment as well as their internal environment. We have spoken in the Introduction of expectations of greater involvement; while technology and size may call for bureaucracy, pressures in society at large may be calling for much looser forms of organisational structure.*

Bennis has predicted an organisational form for the future in the following terms.

> 'The social structure of organisations of the future will have some unique characteristics. The key word will be 'temporary'; there will be adaptive, rapidly changing temporary systems. There will be problem-orientated 'task forces' composed of groups of relative strangers who represent a diverse set of professional skills. The groups will be arranged on an organic rather than a mechanical model; they will evolve in response to a problem rather than to programmed role expectations. The 'executive' thus will become a co-ordinator or 'linking pin' among various task forces. He must be a man who can speak the diverse language

---

*This is but one of many 'contradictions' in the call for participation. Others include instrumental orientations by workers despite improved educational standards seeking to change expectations, situations of 'change and challenge' resisted by managers who prefer to sit it out for their retirement, redesigned jobs which do not produce more job satisfaction, and more job satisfaction which does not produce higher levels of output. Some of these ideas are developed by S. H. Baker and R. A. Hansen, 'Job Design and Worker Satisfaction: A Challenge to Assumptions', *Journal of Occupational Psychology*, Vol. 48, (1975), pp. 79–91.

of research, with skills to relay information and to mediate between groups. People will be differentiated not vertically according to rank and status but flexibly and functionally, according to skill and professional training.

'Adaptive, problem-solving, temporary systems of diverse specialists, linked together by co-ordinating and task-evaluating specialists in an organic flux – this is the organisational form that will gradually replace bureaucracy as we know it.'[1]

If Bennis and other writers such as Argyris[2] and Toffler[3] are correct in their predictions, participation will be justified on the grounds that it is necessary rather than nice.

The world predicted by Bennis and others has perhaps already arrived in those organisations working in advanced technological fields, where the members are predominantly professionals and where the work tends to be characterised by tasks of finite duration rather than a routine unchanging pattern. But not all organisations are, for example, research departments or computer consultancies. As Woodward and Burns and Stalker have pointed out, certain organisational tasks seem to be best suited to organisation structures that lean towards the classical bureaucratic form. Perrow puts the issue bluntly.

'If we want our material civilisation to continue as it is, we will have to have large-scale bureaucratic enterprises in the economic, social and governmental areas. This is the most efficient way to get the routine work done.'[4]

In conclusion then, we must correct any tendency to see this debate – and its obvious implications for participation – in simplistic, either-or terms. At the extremes there will be on one side a need for quite new participative organisations and, on the other, for continuing routine tasks with little opportunity or demand for enrichment. For many organisations in between, there will be conflicting and competing pressures.

We have already noted that within a single organisation there will be departments favouring one style and departments requiring another. This gives rise to problems. The situation, however, can be more complicated than that. Within a single department there are times and tasks appropriate to one and appropriate to another.

A sure foundation of improved relationships and interpersonal trust can carry one over these difficulties. More serious are the ambivalent pressures that organisations will perceive in their environments. Internal and external pressures will not necessarily coincide. Uncertainty calling for participation in one area, will not necessarily be accompanied by legitimacy elsewhere. The world is rarely a coherent, balanced whole. It is a dynamic changing entity in which there are 'lags' and 'leads'.

Organisation cannot simply respond to what is seen to be happening – even if any 'one' pattern could be perceived. Creative administration also makes things happen. Figure 5.1 showed a two-way relationship in which organisations produce changes in their environments as well as needing to respond. The sensible manager will not spend his time fighting unwinnable battles but equally the firm that is truly progressive will not wait for unanimity in its cues from the outside world before taking action. Provided it has taken note of the right cues, the firm that scoops the market will have moved before all the signals show green. But the arguments for participation, unlike other management activities, are not just in terms of effectiveness. The moral issues involved in democracy and job enrichment, for example, could justify action in the face of a totally hostile reaction. Although there are difficulties in reconciling the detail of democratic, quality of life and effectiveness approaches to participation, the overall thrust of all these to greater participation is consistent.

Participation is a long-term process and organisations which wait for the entire complex of variables which affect them to come right, may find that they are only setting out when others are arriving. Many organisations have already read the cues and started taking action; others are just beginning to search out what will be for them the appropriate pathways to participation.

References

1. W.G. Bennis, 'Changing Organisations', *Journal of Applied Behavioural Science,* Vol 2, (1966), pp. 247–63.
2. C. Argyris, 'Today's Problems with Tomorrow's Organisations', *Journal of Management Studies,* Vol 4, (1967), pp. 31–5.
3. A. Toffler, *Future Shock,* The Bodley Head (London 1970).
4. C. Perrow, *Complex Organisations: A Critical Essay,* Scott, Foresman and Company (Brighton 1972), p. 58.

Appendix I Establishing benchmarks for developing participation

A check-list of questions

Where do we stand now on participation as an organisation?	Where would we like to be with regard to participation, as an organisation?
Aspect 1 *Philosophy of participation*	
– How would we describe the prevailing philosophy of participation in the company? – Do we see participation as a worthwhile end in itself or as a means to some other end such as profitability, efficiency, improved morale?	– What philosophy of participation would we like see prevailing in the company? How would we recognise it in practice? What criteria could we use to do this?

- What variations in philosophy can be identified between levels and departments?
- What problems/misunderstandings do they cause?
- How far are the philosophies that people express about participation borne out in the way they behave?
- What do we all mean by 'participation' anyway?

- What do we want to achieve through participation?
- What do we want to achieve as an organisation?

Aspect 2

Participation in practice

- On what issues/areas of decision-making does participation currently take place?
- To what extent does participation take place on these issues? i.e.
  giving information
  consultation
  negotiation
  co-determination
- What machinery do we use to handle participation? e.g. negotiating committees, works councils, briefing groups, etc.

How would we see participative practices within the company changing in response to the changes in philosophy that we would like to see?

- How well does this machinery work in terms of reflecting the company's philosophy of participation, accurately reflecting people's ideas and opinions, encouraging good relationships and producing feasible and acceptable decisions? Is it appropriate to the size, dispersion and structure of the company?

- How satisfied are we with the *extent* to which participation takes place on the various issues subject to participation? e.g. could better decisions be made on some issues if information-giving were extended to consultation?

Aspect 3

People and participation

- Who is involved currently in participation practices within the company?

- Who represents whom on what issues?

- How far do those directly involved

What would be the implications of the changes in our philosophy of participation that we envisage for the skills and attitudes of people involved in participation practices?

as representatives have the required levels of skill to do the job?
– What sort of training do representatives get?
– How far do representatives have the support and resources (e.g. time) that they need for their job?
– How satisfied are those who are represented on various issues by others satisfied with the representation that they get?
– What attitudes do people in the company have to the concept of participation?

Aspect 4

Participation and the internal environment

What are the significant factors in the company's internal environment that have a bearing on participation and how do they have their effect?
e.g.
– organisation size
– organisational structure

What constraints and possibilities do each of these factors present for the way we would like to see participation working in the company?
– Which of them cannot be changed at all?
– Which *could* be changed/

- technology and work processes
- quality of labour relations
- quality of communications
- management control systems
- people's attitudes to and expectations from work
- management styles
- traditional values
- system of rewards

modified?
- Which would *need* to change?
- Which make useful starting points?
- What is best left alone at first?

Aspect 5

Participation and the external environment

What are the significant factors in the company's external environment that have a bearing on participation. What import are they having/are they likely to have?
e.g.
- EEC membership
- recent and possible future Government legislation
- trade unions nationally and locally

- What constraints and possibilities do each of these factors present for the way we would *like* to see participation working in the company?
- Should we regard them all as 'givens' which we can do nothing to influence or *can* we exert some influence?
- What must we *absolutely* do?
- what must we *absolutely* not do?

– social attitudes
– educational trends
– the nature of the market
– organisational implications of the
   product

Appendix II

Bibliography

Aitken H. G. S., *Taylorism at Watertown Arsenal*, Harvard
   University Press (Cambridge 1960).
Alderfer C. P., *Existence, Relatedness, and Growth*, The Free
   Press (New York 1972).
Ansoff I, *Corporate Strategy*, McGraw-Hill (New York 1965).
Anthony P., 'The Coal Industry', in Balfour C., *Participation
   in Industry*, Croom Helm (London 1973).
Argyris C., *Personality and Organisation*, Harper and Row (New
   York 1957).
Argyris C., 'Today's Problems with Tomorrow's
   Organisations,' *Journal of Management Studies*, Vol. 4, (1967)
   31 – 35.
Baker S. H. and Hansen R. A., 'Job Design and Worker
   Satisfaction: A Challenge to Assumptions,' *Journal of
   Occupational Psychology*, Vol. 48, (1975) 79 – 91.
Batstone E. and Davies P. L., *Industrial Democracy: European
   Experience* HMSO (London 1976).
Becker H. S. and Carper J. W., 'The Development of
   Identification with an Occupation', *American Journal of
   Sociology*, Vol. 61, (1956) 289 – 298.
Bendix R., *Work and Authority in Industry*, John Wiley (New
   York 1956).
Bendix R. and Fisher L. H., 'The Perspectives of Elton
   Mayo', *Review of Economics and Statistics*, Vol. 31, (1949),
   312 – 319.

Bennis W. G., 'A Funny Thing Happened on the Way to the Future', in Thomas J. M. and Bennis W. G. (Eds.), *Management of Change and Conflict.* Penguin Books (Harmondsworth 1972).

Bennis W. G., 'Changing Organisations', *Journal of Applied Behavioural Science,* Vol. 2, (1966) 247 – 263.

Beynon H., *Working for Ford,* Penguin Books (Harmondsworth 1973).

Blauner R., *Alienation and Freedom,* Chicago University Press (Chicago 1964).

Blood M. R. and Hulin C., 'Alienation, Environmental Characteristics and Worker Responses', *Journal of Applied Psychology,* Vol. 51, (1967), 284 – 290.

Blumberg P., *Industrial Democracy : The Sociology of Participation,* Constable (London 1968).

Brannen P., Batstone E., Fatchett D., and White P., *The Worker Directors,* Hutchinson (London 1976).

British Institute of Management: Working Party Report, *Front Line Management,* (London 1976).

British Institute of Management, *The Board of Directors,* Management Survey Report No. 10, (London 1972).

Burditt A. R., 'France', in *Worker Participation : The European Experience,* Coventry and District Engineering Employers' Association (Coventry 1974).

Burns T., and Stalker G. M., *The Management of Innovation,* Tavistock (London 1961).

Butteriss M., *Job Enrichment and Employee Participation – A Study,* Institute of Personnel Management (London 1971).

Child J., *British Management Thought,* Allen and Unwin (London 1969).

Clarke R. O., Fatchett D. J., and Roberts B. C., *Workers' Participation in Management in Britain,* Heinemann (London 1972).

Clegg H. A., Killick A. J. and Adams R., *Trade Union Officers,* Blackwell (Oxford 1961).

Coates K. and Topham A., *Industrial Democracy in Great Britain,* MacGibbon and Kee (London 1968).

Coch L. and French J. R. P., Jr, 'Overcoming Resistance to Change', *Human Relations,* Vol. 4, (1948) 512 – 533.

Cole G. D. H., *The Case for Industrial Partnership,* Macmillian (London 1957).

Commission on Industrial Relations, Report No. 33, *Industrial Relations Training,* HMSO (London 1972).

Committee of Inquiry on Industrial Democracy, *Report,* HMSO (London 1977).

Communist Part of Great Britain, *Evidence to the Committee of Inquiry on Industrial Democracy,* (London 1976).

Cotgtove S., Dunham J, and Vanplew C., *The Nylon Spinners,* Allen and Unwin (London 1971).

Coveney A., 'Olsen's Democracy', *Industrial Society,* (Nov. – Dec. 1975) 11 – 13.

Dalton M., *Men who Manage,* John Wiley (New York 1959).

Daniel W. W. and McIntosh N., *The Right to Manage?* Macdonald (London 1972).

Duerr C., *Draft Interim Report on the Worker Director: How it works at Bonser Engineering Limited* (October 1975).

Duerr C., *Management Kinetics,* McGraw–Hill (Maidenhead 1971).

Edgren J., *With Varying Success – A Swedish Experiment in Wage Systems and Shop Floor Organisation.* Swedish Employers' Confederation (Stockholm 1974).

European Communities Commission, *Employee Participation and Company Structure* (Luxembourg 1975).

Flanders A., Pomeranz R., and Woodward J., *Experiment in Industrial Democracy,* Faber and Faber (London 1968).

Flanders A., *Collective Bargaining: Prescription for Change,* Faber and Faber (London 1967).

Flanders A., *The Fawley Productivity Agreements,* Faber and Faber (London 1964).

Flanders A., *Industrial Relations: What is wrong with the System,* Faber and Faber (London 1965).

Fox A., 'Industrial Relations: A Social Critique of Pluralist Ideology', in Child J. (Ed.) *Man and Organisation: The Search for Explanation and Social Relevance,* Allen and Unwin (London 1973).

Fox A., *Industrial Sociology and Industrial Relations,* Royal Commission on Trade Unions and Employers' Associations, Research Paper No. 3, HMSO (London 1966).

Fox A., *A Sociology of Work in Industry,* Collier–Macmillan (London 1971).

Fox A., *Man Mismanagement,* Hutchinson, (London, 1974).

French J.R.P., Israel J. and As D., 'An Experiment on Participation in a Norwegian Factory', *Human Relations,* Vol. 13, (1960) 3 – 19.

Fûrstenburg F., 'Workers' Participation in Management in the Federal Republic of Germany', *International Institute for Labour Studies Bulletin* Vol. 6, (1969), 94 – 148.

Garnier T., 'Case Studies in Humanised Management: The Kalamazoo Workers' Alliance', *Industrial and Commercial Training,* (July 1976) 260 – 264.

Goldthorpe J. H., Lockwood D., Bechhoffer P., and Platt J., *The Affluent Worker: Industrial Attitudes and Behaviour,* Cambridge University Press (Cambridge 1968).

Government Social Survey, *Workplace Industrial Relations,* HMSO (London 1968).

Guest D. and Fatchett D., *Worker Participation: Individual Control and Performance,* Institute of Personal Management (London 1974).

Harrison R., *Workers' Participation in Western Europe 1976,* Institute of Personnel Management (London 1976).

Hebden J. E., 'Patterns of Work Identification', *Sociology of Work and Occupations,* Vol. 2 (1975) 107 – 132.

Hebden J. E., Rose M. J., and Scott W. H., 'Management Structure and Computerisation', *Sociology,* Vol. 3, (Sept. 1969) 377 – 396.

Homans G. C., 'Some Corrections to the "The Perspectives of Elton Mayo," ' *Review of Economics and Statistics,* Vol. 31, (1949) 319 – 321.

Hyman R., *Industrial Relations: A Marxist Introduction*

Macmillan (London 1975).

Ingham G. K., *Size of Industrial Organisation and Worker Behaviour,* Cambridge University Press (Cambridge 1970).

International Labour Organisation, *Co-operation in Industry* (Geneva 1951).

Jackson P., 'The Supervisor and Techological Change – A Study of the Changing Role of the Supervisor in the Port Transport Industry,' *Occasional Papers No. 1* National Ports Council (London 1970).

Jacques E., *The Changing Culture of a Factory,* Tavistock (London 1951).

Katz D., Maccoby N., Gurin G., and Floor L. G. *Productivity, Supervision and Morale among Railroad Workers,* Survey Research Center, Institute for Social Research, University of Michigan (Ann Arbor 1951).

Katz D., Maccoby N., and Morse N. C., *Productivity, Supervision and Morale in an Office Situation,* Survey Research Center, Institute for Social Research, University of Michigan (Ann Arbor 1950).

King Taylor L., *Not for Bread Alone,* Business Books (London 1973).

King Taylor L., 'Participation without Patronising', *Industrial and Commercial Training* (May 1973) 211 – 215.

Kuhn J. W., *Bargaining in Grievance Settlement* Columbia University Press (New York 1961).

Lawler E. E. III and Porter L., 'Antecedent Attitudes of Effective Managerial Performance' in Vroom V and Deci E. L., (Eds.) *Management and Motivation,* Penguin Books, (Harmondsworth, 1970).

Lawrence P. R., and Lorsch J. W., *Organisation and Environment,* Harvard University Press (Cambridge 1967).

Lewin K., 'Group Decision and Social Change', in Newcombe T. M. and Hartley E. L., *Readings in Social Psychology,* Henry Holt (New York 1953).

Lewin K., *Resolving Social Conflicts,* Souvenir Press (London 1973).

Likert R., *The Human Organisation,* McGraw–Hill (New York 1967).

Likert R., *New Patterns of Management,* McGraw–Hill, (New York, 1961).

Lippitt G. L., and Seashore E. W., 'The Leader Looks at Group Effectiveness'. *Looking into Leadership Monographs,* Leadership Resources Inc. (Washington DC 1961).

Lovelady L. "Workplace Democratisation – Problems at the Union – Management Interface', from a forthcoming collection of papers in preparation by the International Quality of Working Life Committee.

Marsh A. I., *Dispute Procedure in British Industry,* Royal Commission on Trade Unions and Employers' Associations, Research Paper No. 2, HMSO (London 1966).

Maslow A. H., *Motivation and Personality,* Harper and Row (New York 1954).

McCarthy W. E. S. and Ellis N. D., *Management by Agreement: An alternative to the Industrial Relations Act,* Hutchinson (London 1973).

McCarthy W. E. S., and Parker S. R., *Shop Stewards and Workshop Relations,* Royal Commission on Trade Unions and Employers' Associations, Research Paper No. 10, HMSO (London 1968).

McGivering I., Matthews D., and Scott W. H., *Management in Britain* Liverpool University Press (Liverpool 1960).

McGregor D., *The Human Side of Enterprise,* McGraw–Hill (New York 1960).

Morrison H., *Socialisation and Transport* Constable (London 1933).

Morse N. C., and Reimer E., 'The Experimental Change of a Major Organisational Variable' *Journal of Abnormal and Social Psychology* Vol. 52 (1956) 120–129.

National Institute of Industrial Psychology, *Joint Consultation in British Industry,* Staples Press (London 1951).

Nichols T., *Ownership, Control and Ideology* Allen and Unwin (London 1969).

Norstedt J. P. and Agurén S., *The Saab-Scania Report*, Swedish
    Employers' Confederation (Stockholm 1973).
O'Brian E., 'Plant Procedure and Agreements: A Case
    Study', in Kessler S., and Weekes B., (Eds.), *Conflict at Work,*
    BBC Publications (London 1971).
Opinion Research Centre, *What about the Workers?'* Dragonfly
    Publications (London 1975).
Pahl R. E., and Winkler J. T., 'The Economic Elite: Theory
    and Practice', in Stanworth P., and Giddens A. (Eds.), *Elites
    and Power in British Society,* Cambridge University Press
    (London 1974).
Paul W. S., and Robertson K. B., *Job Enrichment and Employee
    Motivation,* Gower Press (London 1971).
Pelz D. C., 'Influence: A Key to Effective Leadership in the
    First Line Supervisor', *Personnel* Vol. 29, (1952) 209 – 217.
Perrow C., *Complex Organisations: A Critical Essay,* Scott,
    Foresman (Brighton 1972).
Pigors P. and Myers C. A., *Personnel Administration,*
    McGraw–Hill (London 1961).
Poole M., *Workers' Participation in Industry,* Routledge and
    Kegan Paul (London 1975).
Roberts B. C., *Industrial Democracy – The Challenge to
    Management* Institute of Personnel Management, National
    Conference (October 1976).
Roethlisberger F. J., The Foreman: Master and Victim of
    Double Talk, *Harvard Business Review,* Vol. 23, (1945) 285 –
    294.
Roethlisberger F. J. and Dickson W. J., *Management and the
    Worker,* John Wiley (New York 1964).
Royal Commission on Trade Unions and Employers'
    Associations, *Report,* HMSO (London 1968).
Sayles L. R., and Strauss G., *Human Behavior in Organisations,*
    Prentice – Hall (Englewood Cliffs 1966).
Schumacher E. F., *Small is Beautiful,* Blond and Briggs
    (London 1973).
Scott W. H., *Industrial Leadership and Joint Consultation,*

Liverpool University Press (Liverpool 1952).

Scott W. H., Banks J. A., Halsey A. H., and Lupton T., *Technical Change and Industrial Relations,* Liverpool University Press (Liverpool 1956).

Starbuck W. H., *Organisational Growth and Development,* Penguin Books (Harmondsworth 1971).

Strauss G., 'Group Dynamics and Intergroup Relations', in Whyte W. F., *Money and Motivation,* Harper and Row (London 1955).

Strauss G., 'Participative Management: A Critique', *ILR Research* Vol. 12, (1966) 3 – 6.

Swedish Employers' Confederation, *Job Reform in Sweden,* (Stockholm 1975).

Swedish Employers' Confederation, *The Volvo Report,* (Stockholm 1975).

Tannenbaum A. S., *Control in Organisations,* McGraw–Hill (New York 1968).

Tannenbaum A. S., *Social Psychology of the Work Organisation,* Tavistock (London 1973).

Taylor F. W. *The Principles of Scientific Management,* Harper and Row (New York 1911).

Taylor N., Time to Prepare for Participation, *Personnel Management,* Vol. 8 (August 1976) 3.

Thomason G. F. *Experiments in Participation,* Institute of Personnel Management (London 1971).

Thomason G. F. 'Workers' Participation in Private Enterprise Organisations', in Balfour C., *Participation in Industry,* Croom Helm (London 1973).

Tilden W. A., 'Germany' in *Worker Participation: The European Experience,* Coventry and District Engineering Employers' Association (Coventry 1974).

Toffler A., *Future Shock,* The Bodley Head (London 1970).

Topham A. 'A Four Point Policy for the Unions', *Tribune,* 25 February 1966.

Trist E. L. and Bamforth K. W., 'Some Social and Psychological Consequences of the Longwall Method of

Coal Getting'. *Human Relations,* Vol. 4, (1951) 3 – 38.

Turner A. N. and Lawrence P. R. *Industrial Jobs and the Worker,* Harvard University Press (Boston 1965).

Vroom V., *Work and Motivation,* John Wiley (New York 1964).

Walker C. R., and Guest R. H., *Man on the Assembly Line,* Yale University Press (New Haven 1957).

Walton R. E., 'How to counter Alienation in the Plant', *Harvard Business Review,* (Nov–Dec. 1972).

Walton R. E., and McKersie R. B., *A Behavioral Theory of Labor Negotiations* McGraw–Hill (New York 1965).

Wellens J., 'Comments on the KWA Scheme,' *Industrial and Commercial Training* (July 1976) 265 – 268.

Wellens J., *Worker Participation: A Practical Policy,* Wellens Publishing (Guilsborough 1975).

White R., and Lippitt R., *Autocracy and Democracy: An Experimental Enquiry* Harper and Row (New York 1960).

Whitehead T. N., *Leadership in a Free Society,* Oxford University Press (Oxford 1936).

Woodward J., *Industrial Organisation: Theory and Practice,* Oxford University Press (London 1965).

Index

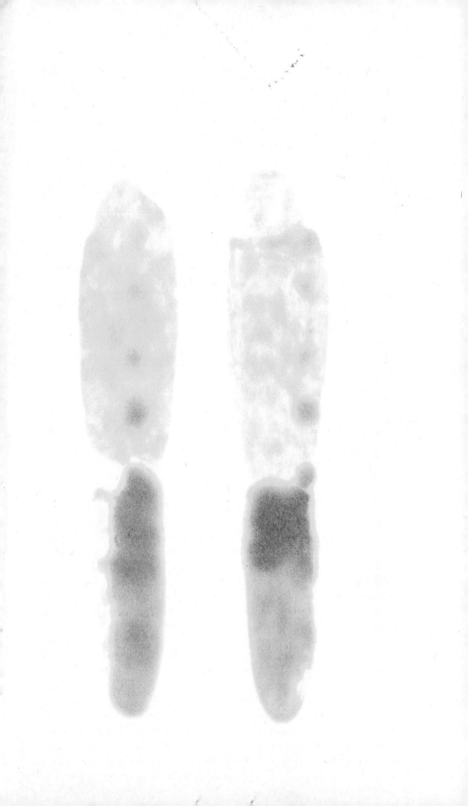